The Bible
Unwrapped

Developing
your Bible skills

DAVID DEWEY
Scripture Union

Scripture Union, 207–209 Queensway, Bletchley, MK2 2EB, England

Email: info@scriptureunion.org.uk
Web site: www.scriptureunion.org.uk

First published 2001
ISBN 1 85999 533 0

British Library Cataloguing-in-Publication Data.
A catalogue record of this book is available from the British Library.

Printed and bound in Great Britain by Creative Print and Design (Wales) Ebbw Vale.

Scripture Union is an international Christian charity working with churches in more than 130 countries providing resources to bring the good news about Jesus Christ to children, young people and families – and to encourage them to develop spiritually through the Bible and prayer.

As well as our network of volunteers, staff and associates who run holidays, church-based events and school Christian groups, we produce a wide range of publications and support those who use our resources through training programmes.

Contents

All Scripture references are from the New International Version (inclusive language edition) unless otherwise stated.

Dedication

To Ann Hicks (1953–2000),
whose faith triumphed over
her breast cancer, now with
the Lord and enjoying a
perfect resurrection body.

Welcome

I OFTEN thank God for the Earl of Surrey. I have never met his lordship, but he made sure every boy in my school was given his own Bible. It was a Revised Standard Version with plenty of 'thees' and 'thous', but nowhere near as many as in the old black dust-covered Bible in my parents' bookcase.

Some of the Bibles got torn up; some were used as missiles when our teacher had his back to the class. More out of curiosity than anything else, I took mine home. I began reading – at the beginning as one does with a normal book. A mistake. The Bible is no normal book.

Genesis wasn't too bad: I had vaguely heard of characters like Noah and Joseph, but I must confess to skipping through the long lists of unpronounceable names. But I came unstuck in Exodus, with its spontaneously combusting bushes, gruesome plagues and long chapters full of measurements and materials for a tabernacle – a tent for open-air worship as far as I could make out.

I gave up and the Bible languished in my desk, brought out for just the odd RE lesson. Then, through the witness of friends in the school Christian Union, I was introduced to Jesus Christ. I became a Christian. Two things happened with that Bible. First, it started to make sense in a way it had never done before. There was still plenty I couldn't understand – and some parts I still don't! – but it came alive. It was about someone I knew. It was about Jesus Christ, my Saviour; it was about God the Father

I talked with in prayer; it was about the Holy Spirit at work in my life.

Second, I found myself hungry to read more. The more I read, the more I wanted to read. Bible reading notes gave me a passage to study each day and helped me understand what I was reading. I took my Bible to church so I could follow as the pastor preached from the pulpit. And joining a young people's Bible study group gave me the opportunity of discussing what I was learning with others.

My once pristine Bible soon started to look quite tatty. But it didn't matter. A closed book was now an open book. And that was exciting.

⚭

I cannot make the Bible come alive to you as it came alive to me. That's between you and the Holy Spirit. But I hope I can whet your appetite and give you some of the skills and tools that make the task of Bible reading easier and more rewarding.

There are many introductions to the Bible available. I will recommend some in chapter 9. But the great danger is you will read them and not the Bible itself. People are always looking for shortcuts: *Hungarian in Six Weeks, Cordon Bleu Cookery with One Saucepan, Brain Surgery in Three Simple Steps* or *The Bible Made Dead Easy*. The Bible is not 'dead easy', but uncovering the truth it contains is the most important thing you will ever do.

The purpose of *The Bible Unwrapped* is to get you into the Bible and the Bible into you. It will tell you some facts about the Bible and it will introduce you to its contents, but what it will concentrate on are the *skills* of Bible reading and study – skills that will set you up for a lifetime of growth as a disciple of Jesus Christ.

Chapters 1–4 should be tackled first and in order. The first two chapters take an introductory look at the Bible; chapter 3 looks at some basic approaches to Bible reading; and chapter 4 sets out a timeline of Bible history. Chapters 5 and 6 then take you deeper in Bible reading skills. Chapters 7–10 are for reference: dip into these as you need more information. Altogether, we will consider eight different approaches to reading and studying the Bible. These are found in chapters 3, 5 and 6.

All the time I'll be pointing you to parts of the Bible you can read for yourself. So, as you work your way through this book, be sure to have a Bible close at hand. For now, any Bible will do, but I'd recommend a modern translation – one with 'you' and 'yours', not 'thee' and 'thine'. Chapter 9 has information about different versions and other useful resources.

Although the Bible is not an easy book, I don't want you to think that it is a difficult book which only someone with a PhD-intellect can understand. Yes, God wants us to use our brains and stretch our minds, but the Bible is not unlocked by the power of intelligence. It is opened by the illumination of the Spirit. That doesn't mean putting our thought processes and critical faculties on hold, but it does mean opening ourselves – heart and mind – to spiritual truth.

Spiritual truth is spiritually understood (1 Corinthians 2:14). The simplest soul and the youngest child, if they are open to God, can get as much as anyone else from reading the Bible, and feasting on God's Word, yet the greatest scholar will always have more to learn. William Tyndale, who in 1536 was burnt at the stake for his work in translating the Bible into English, once said to a scholar who opposed his efforts: 'Before long, if God spares my life, I will make sure that a mere ploughboy knows Scripture better than you.' Psalm 119 verse 18 offers a prayer: 'Open my eyes that I may see wonderful things in your law.'

Bible references

Before you go any further you'll need to know how Bible references work. If you are already confident in finding your way around the Bible, skip to chapter 1. If not, here's an example of how to decipher a Scripture reference:

2 Timothy 3:16

There are three parts to this reference: the book name, the chapter number and, finally, the verse. In this case the book is 2 Timothy (pronounced either Two or Second Timothy). To give it its full title, it is Paul's Second Letter to Timothy. It is a short book located towards the end of your Bible. If you can't find it – it is only a few pages long – the contents list in your Bible will give you the page number.

The rest is straightforward. 2 Timothy is divided into four chapters. We want chapter 3. And the last part of the reference points us to verse 16. If you have found the correct place, it will say this: 'All Scripture is God-breathed and is useful for teaching, rebuking, correcting and training in righteousness.'

Don't worry if your Bible uses slightly different words. I've quoted from the New International Version. If you are using a different Bible, that's fine. In the New Living Translation the same verse says: 'All Scripture is inspired by God and is useful to teach us what is true and to make us realise what is wrong in our lives. It straightens us out and teaches us to do what is right.'

Different words, same meaning. This verse tells us the Bible is God's inspired and living Word; that it is utterly reliable and absolutely essential for all aspects of Christian growth.

Points to watch

When looking up Bible references, there are extra points to watch:

• Some books share the same name. Timothy is one example.

Because the apostle Paul wrote two letters to his young friend, we have both First and Second Timothy. In the Old Testament the reason for numbering certain books First and Second (ie Samuel, Kings and Chronicles) is different. They've been split only because of their length: each was originally one unbroken book.

- Abbreviations are often used for the books of the Bible. See the list below, or the one in your Bible.

- Other common abbreviations include: 'ch' for chapter; 'v' for verse (and 'vv' or 'vs' for verses); 'f' or 'ff' means 'and following' (so 2 Tim 3:16f is the same as 2 Tim 3:16,17); and 'cp' or 'cf' means 'compare with'.

Bible books and their abbreviations

Books in the Old Testament

Genesis	Gen	2 Chronicles	2 Chr	Daniel	Dan
Exodus	Exod	Ezra	Ezra	Hosea	Hos
Leviticus	Lev	Nehemiah	Neh	Joel	Joel
Numbers	Num	Esther	Esth	Amos	Amos
Deuteronomy	Deut	Job	Job	Obadiah	Obad
Joshua	Josh	Psalms	Ps	Jonah	Jonah
Judges	Judg	Proverbs	Prov	Micah	Mic
Ruth	Ruth	Ecclesiastes	Eccl	Nahum	Nah
1 Samuel	1 Sam	Song of Songs	Song	Habakkuk	Hab
2 Samuel	2 Sam	Isaiah	Isa	Zephaniah	Zeph
1 Kings	1 Kings	Jeremiah	Jer	Haggai	Hag
2 Kings	2 Kings	Lamentations	Lam	Zechariah	Zech
1 Chronicles	1 Chr	Ezekiel	Ezek	Malachi	Mal

Books in the New Testament

Matthew	Matt	Ephesians	Eph	Hebrews	Heb
Mark	Mark	Philippians	Phil	James	James
Luke	Luke	Colossians	Col	1 Peter	1 Pet
John	John	1 Thessalonians	1 Thess	2 Peter	2 Pet
Acts	Acts	2 Thessalonians	2 Thess	1 John	1 John
Romans	Rom	1 Timothy	1 Tim	2 John	2 John
1 Corinthians	1 Cor	2 Timothy	2 Tim	3 John	3 John
2 Corinthians	2 Cor	Titus	Titus	Jude	Jude
Galatians	Gal	Philemon	Philemon	Revelation	Rev

The Old Testament (abbreviated to OT) contains thirty-nine books, found in the first part of the Bible. They were written before the time of Christ. The New Testament (NT), in the second part of the Bible, has twenty-seven books covering the life of Christ and the story of the early Christian church.

1

'Let me introduce you...'

God's words are more precious than gold,
than much pure gold;
they are sweeter than honey,
than honey from the comb (Ps 19:10)

AT A PARTY, you see someone you'd like to meet and get to
know. But how are you going to strike up an acquaintance? A
mutual friend steps in: 'Let me introduce you.' Introductions
are made: 'Rachel, this is Brian. He works in the offices over the
road.' And vice versa. But once the introductions are done, it is
over to you.

And that is the purpose of this book: to introduce you to the
Bible. It will not tell you all you want or need to know, and it is
certainly no substitute for your own personal exploration of the
Bible. It is simply to help break the ice, to give you pointers as
to what the Bible is all about, how it fits together and how it can
best be read, understood and applied.

In attempting to unwrap the Bible and to understand how it
works in our lives, it's important to understand what it is and
what it is not.

It is about God
It may sound self-evident to say the Bible is about God. Of course
it is, but we need to understand *in what way* it is about God.

> The secret things belong to the Lord our God, but the things revealed belong to us and to our children forever, that we may follow all the words of this law (Deut 29:29).

> Now we see but a poor reflection as in a mirror; then we shall see face to face. Now I know in part; then I shall know fully, even as I am fully known (1 Cor 13:12).

God cannot be examined in the way a scientist might scrutinise a laboratory specimen. For one thing, God is living and eternal (Jer 10:10). For another, he is beyond the capabilities of the human mind to fathom (Job 11:7; Ps 145:3; Eccl 3:11). And for yet another, he can be known only through *revelation*: what we know of God is only what God chooses to make known.

The Bible is a book of revelation. It reveals God. But it does so through a series of snatched glimpses. Imagine being in a car and driving along a hedge-lined road. An occasional break in the hedge or a farm gate reveals the view beyond. Once you've passed several such breaks, you begin to build up a mental picture of the hidden panorama. One gap reveals a hill; the next shows a river by the hill; the next a house by the river. And so on, extending the picture each time. There are some bits you never get to see; there are other parts you see several times over.

But the view also changes as you drive along. Some parts drop out of sight while new elements come into view. Certain features, like a distant mountain, are constant but other elements change. And even the mountain changes slightly. A bend in the road will bring a new perspective. Same mountain, new angle.

The revelation of God we find in the Bible is like that. It is *progressive* and *accumulative*. There is only one God and he never changes (Ps 102:27; Heb 13:8; James 1:17). But as the Bible unfolds, our understanding of God develops and grows. But the full picture, the unobscured view, will be apparent only when we see the Lord 'face to face' (1 Cor 13:12).

It is about salvation

While the Bible cannot tell us everything about God – there are aspects of his character and purpose that must remain a mystery to our limited minds – it does tell us everything we need in order to find salvation through Jesus Christ. Paul says to Timothy: 'You have known the holy Scriptures, which are able to make you wise for salvation through faith in Christ Jesus' (2 Tim 3:15).

The story of the Bible is the story of God's unfolding plan of salvation, the revelation of his love to a rebellious humankind that has lost its way. It is about our personal salvation and it is about God's plan of restoration for a fallen, sin-damaged universe.

The opening scene is creation. From the vastness of the cosmos, the focus narrows to planet Earth and the creation of humankind. Then we see the effects of human disobedience casting a shadow over all God has made and declared 'good'.

From Adam the story moves on to Abraham. He is the father of Israel, humanly speaking an insignificant nation, but chosen by God as his vehicle of revelation and salvation. Stories of Israel's changing fortunes occupy the Old Testament.

Again the story narrows: to Jesus Christ, God's Son and the world's Saviour. God's salvation is no longer the near-exclusive property of the Jews but is open to all, Jew and non-Jew alike. After Christ's resurrection, we have the outpouring of the Holy Spirit (Acts 2), the day the Church is born. And from New Testament times until the present, it is the Church that is the carrier of the Good News of God's saving work through Christ.

We'll consider the big picture of the Bible further in chapter 4. But for now, we rejoice in the simple truth that the Bible – because it points us to Jesus Christ – contains all we need to know for spiritual new birth: 'For you have been born again, not of perishable seed, but of imperishable, through the living and enduring word of God' (1 Pet 1:23). And having been born again, it is God's Word that helps us grow from infancy to maturity in Christ: 'Like newborn babies, crave pure spiritual milk, so that by it you may grow up in your salvation, now that you have tasted that the Lord is good' (1 Pet 2:2,3).

It is about us

The Bible reveals God's nature and his *plan of salvation*. It also reveals human nature and *our need of salvation*. It is as much about us as it is about God. It depicts human nature warts and all. Most especially, it reveals the state of the human heart – cut off from God by sin and in need of a Saviour.

In the New Testament, James compares God's Word with a mirror:

> Those who listen to the Word but do not do what it says are like people who look at their faces in a mirror and, after looking at themselves, go away and immediately forget what they look like. But those who look intently into the perfect law that gives freedom, and continue to do this, not forgetting what they have heard, but doing it – they will be blessed in what they do (James 1:23–25).

Reading the Bible is like looking into a reflection. All human life is on display, from the noblest achievements to which humankind can aspire, to the very worst examples of human depravity. The human condition is laid bare in the Bible. Fallen human nature is exposed – my human nature is exposed. My inner motives and thoughts bounce back from the pages of scripture. And it is not always a pretty sight.

To the Old Testament prophet Jeremiah, God describes his Word in another way: '"Is not my word like fire," declares the Lord, "and like a hammer that breaks a rock in pieces?"' (Jer 23:29). When my heart is hard like stone, God's Word has the power to break through the defences I raise against him. The Bible can – and often does – bring the toughest and roughest to their knees before God.

Sometimes the Bible explodes like a bombshell, but sometimes its truth slices deeply and deliberately like a scalpel in the hands of a skilled surgeon. God's Word pierces the innermost depths of our humanity:

> The word of God is full of living power. It is sharper than the sharpest knife, cutting deep into our innermost thoughts and desires. It exposes us for what we really are. Nothing in all creation can hide from him. Everything is naked and exposed before his eyes. This is the God to whom we must explain all we have done (Heb 4:12,13, NLT).

As well as uncovering what lies deep inside the human soul, God's Word also mends. It gives life. It heals, soothes and nourishes: 'Jesus said, "It is written: 'You do not live on bread alone, but on every word that comes from the mouth of God'"' (Matt 4:4). When Jesus said this, he was quoting the Old Testament (from Deut 8:3) in his defence against Satan who was tempting him to turn stones into bread. The point Jesus was making is that while physical food feeds our bodies, the bread of God's Word is vital for feeding our souls.

Psalm 1 introduces the Book of Psalms with these lines:

> Blessed are those
>   who do not walk in the counsel of the wicked
> or stand in the way of sinners
>   or sit in the seat of mockers.
> But their delight is in the law of the Lord,
>   and on his law they meditate day and night.
> They are like trees planted by streams of water
>   which yield their fruit in season
> and whose leaves do not wither.
>   Whatever they do prospers.

A tree close to a reliable water source will be firm and secure, its roots deep and strong. It will receive constant refreshment:

even under a scorching sun its leaves won't droop. Most importantly, it will bear fruit. The Christian who is firmly and deeply rooted in God's Word will be equally healthy.

Less poetically, in a verse we've already met, Paul says this: 'All Scripture is God-breathed. It is good for teaching the truth and refuting error; for correcting wrong behaviour and training in right behaviour' (2 Tim 3:16, author's translation). Scripture, says Paul, offers a four-way benefit. It promotes both right belief and right behaviour. It does each of these two things through both positive and negative means:

Through example and warning, command and prohibition,

	Positive	**Negative**
Belief	Teaches truth	Refutes error
Behaviour	Trains in the right ways	Corrects our wrong ways

God's Word trains the Christian both to think according to God's truth and to live according to God's ways.

It is about Jesus Christ

The Bible is about God's nature and it is about human nature. It is also – supremely –about the One who is both God and Man. It is about Jesus Christ.

Well, you may say, I can see that the Gospels and much of the New Testament are about Jesus Christ but that is less than a quarter of the Bible. What about the Old Testament? How can that be about him?

Luke records what Jesus said to his disciples when he appeared to them after the resurrection: 'This is what I told you while I was still with you: "Everything must be fulfilled that is written about me in the Law of Moses, the Prophets and the Psalms." Then he opened their minds so they could understand the Scriptures' (Luke 24:44,45).

The Jews divide their Bible – what Christians now call the Old Testament – into three: the Law, the Prophets and the Writings. The first and longest book in the Writings is the Book of Psalms. So Jesus' description of 'the Law of Moses, the Prophets and the Psalms' was his way of referring to the entire Old Testament! It must have been some Bible study! Unfortunately, its full content is not recorded. But we do know he explained to them how his death and resurrection had taken place in fulfilment of Old Testament prediction: 'He told them, "This is what is written: The Christ will suffer and rise from the dead on the third day, and repentance and forgiveness of sins will be preached in his name to all nations, beginning at Jerusalem"' (Luke 24:46,47; compare Acts 17:2,3; 26:22,23; 28:23; 1 Cor 15:3,4).

On an earlier occasion, Jesus was addressing his scholarly opponents: 'You diligently study the Scriptures because you think that by them you possess eternal life. These are the Scriptures that testify about me, yet you refuse to come to me to have life' (John 5:39,40). Although these scholars studied the Old Testament in detail all their lives, they failed to see that the Scriptures pointed to Jesus Christ. Over 300 Old Testament prophecies look forward to the birth, life, death and resurrection of Jesus. A selection is given in chapter 10.

The central figure of the Bible is Jesus Christ, God's most perfect revelation of himself – God made Man, God in human form. The Old Testament anticipates him and finds its fulfilment in him; the Gospels record his life and teaching; and the rest of the New Testament shows how salvation is available only through him.

When we come to the Bible, we come not only to *read* about God and Jesus Christ, we come to meet God through Jesus Christ. The written Word takes us to Jesus Christ, the living and eternal Word (see John 1:1,14).

What the Bible is not

1. The Bible is not a book of systematic doctrine

Although the Bible is the authority by which the Church establishes Christian doctrine, it is not a book of doctrine or theology as such. Doctrine is the systematic and orderly setting out of Christian truth. Only on rare occasions does the Bible come anywhere close to doing this. Mostly the Bible is a pretty disorderly and unsystematic record of human experience of God and God's experience of human beings. The Bible does not even attempt to prove the existence of God. It simply starts: 'In the beginning God' – and goes on from there.

2. The Bible is not a book of simple history

Although the Bible contains plenty of history, it is not a straightforward history book. Its history, although reliable, is selective and written for the purpose of revealing God and encouraging faith. The biblical authors chose to write from a particular perspective: it is sacred – or spiritual – history, focusing on God's dealings with his people. Details other chroniclers of history would count as important are barely mentioned while people and events that most historians would dismiss out of hand are given greater prominence. After all, Jesus, a mere carpenter from the backwater of Galilee, turns out to be the Bible's central character.

3. The Bible is not a book of magic or secret codes

Although the Bible offers power for living, it is not a book of magic. Incanting the right verse at the right time will not make a traffic jam dissipate before your eyes. Although divinely inspired (2 Tim 3:16), it did not drop from heaven. God did not dictate it word by word through people acting as hypnotised typists with their minds and personalities temporarily

disengaged. For the most part, those who wrote the Bible –
some 40 authors in all – had no idea they were penning
scripture.

John Stott speaks of the dual authorship of scripture when
he says that 'the Bible is equally the Word of God and the word
of men.' Comparing the Bible with Christ, he continues: 'There
is ... such a combination of the divine and the human that we
must affirm each without denying the other... We must neither
affirm [the Bible's] divine origin in such a way as to deny the
free activity of the human authors, nor affirm their active co-
operation in such a way as to deny that through them God
spoke his word.'[1]

Nor does the Bible contain secret codes or hidden messages
which can be unlocked only by scholars, the specially initiated
or the deeply holy. Its meaning is plain to all who come to it
with an open mind and a searching heart.

4. The Bible is not a book at all!
And on top of all this, the Bible is not really a book at all! It
doesn't have a beginning, middle and end like other books. It is
a whole set of different books, written in very different styles.
While putting the sixty-six separate books of the Bible in one
cover makes life more convenient, the Bible is really a diverse
library of books, books that one wouldn't find anywhere near
each other in any conventional collection.

There are books of prose and of poetry; books of biography,
family sagas, census records, royal records, accounts of war,
battle songs, prayers and hymns, prophecies and visions, legal
documents, architectural designs, temple inventories, home-
spun philosophy, moral debates, pithy one-line proverbs, mem-
oirs, family trees, personal letters and even some rather juicy
love poetry (yes, really! – Song of Songs can give the *Kama
Sutra* a run for its money!).

We can think of the Bible as a jigsaw, made up of many different kinds of writing:

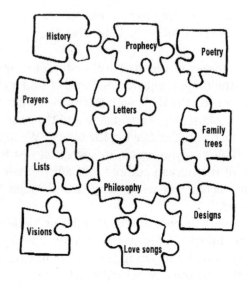

A translation

The Bible you have in your hands is a translation. The Old Testament was written almost entirely in Hebrew, a language written and read from right to left. It originally had no vowels, only consonants. You probably know at least three Hebrew words: 'hallelujah' – 'praise the Lord'; 'amen' – 'so be it'; and 'shalom' – 'peace'.

The New Testament was written in Greek, the common language of the Roman Empire in the first century AD. One Greek word you may know is *agapé* – God's unconditional love towards us and the kind of selfless love Christians are to show to one another.

Jesus probably knew both Hebrew and Greek, but his everyday tongue was Aramaic, a sister language of Hebrew. A few brief sections of the Old Testament (in Ezra and Daniel) are in Aramaic, and a few isolated words of it are also found scattered in the New Testament. One Aramaic word is *Abba*, meaning 'Father' (Mark 14:36, Rom 8:15).

How the Bible describes itself

> As the rain and the snow come down from heaven, and do
> not return to it without watering the earth and making it
> bud and flourish, so that it yields seed for the sower and
> bread for the eater, so is my word that goes out from my
> mouth: it will not return to me empty, but will accomplish
> what I desire and achieve the purpose for which I sent it
> (Isa 55:10,11).

The Bible describes itself in a number of ways. We've already
met a few of them. Here are three more. This time, you look up
the references for yourself:

Seed (Mark 4:3–8, 13–20)

This powerful parable describes the sowing of God's word in the
human heart. It is worth pondering the various categories.
What hinders God's word in your life? Where is it bearing fruit?

Light (Psalm 119:105)

God's word directs and guides.

Sword (Ephesians 6:17)

God's word is like a Roman soldier's sword, a part of the
Christian's armour worn in battle against Satan, our spiritual
enemy. God's truth, treasured in our hearts, protects against
temptation (see Ps 119:11). Read how Jesus used scripture in
his battle with the devil in Matthew 4:1–11.

'Apply regularly'

Sun block cream is of no use in the tube. Neither is the Bible
any use unless it is read regularly and applied liberally. You
could memorise the entire Bible by heart, but unless it makes a
difference, you would have wasted your time. The Bible is not
given to *inform*, but to *transform*. Steve Motyer writes: 'It is not
just a source of information about God; it is also a source of

power, which really can change us if we will be open to it.'[2] And James reminds us: 'Do not merely listen to the word, and so deceive yourselves. Do what it says' (James 1:22).

New Zealander Mike Riddell knows how to tell a story with a sharp point:

> A great explorer returned to her people after a long expedition. They were eager to know all about her adventures, and in particular about the mighty Amazon which she had travelled... But how could she speak of the feelings which had flooded her heart when she saw the exotic flowers and heard the mighty sounds of the forests; when she sensed the dangers of the wild beasts or paddled her canoe over treacherous rapids?
>
> She said to the people, 'Go and find out for yourselves.' To guide them she drew a map of the river. They pounced upon the map. They framed it in their town hall. They made copies of it for themselves. They studied it night and day and became experts in interpreting the river. They knew its every turn and bend, they knew how broad it was, how deep, where the rapids and waterfalls were. And yet, not one of them ever left the village to see for themselves.[3]

The Bible is not for armchair travellers, but for adventurers. And in the next chapter the adventure begins in earnest.

[1] John Stott, *Evangelical Truth*, IVP, 1999, pages 56-61.
[2] Steve Motyer, *The Bible with Pleasure*, revised edition, Crossway Books (IVP), 1997, p12.
[3] Mike Riddell, *Godzone*, Lion Publishing, 1992, pages 72,73.

2

Beyond first impressions

FIRST impressions count, but they are never the whole story. They can even mislead. In this chapter we'll try to get beyond whatever first impressions of the Bible you might have; we're going to delve deeper and begin a personal exploration.

Whatever else you think of the Bible, you'll know by now it is a big book. That particular first impression is without doubt true. The Bible has just over three-quarters of a million words (774,746 in the Authorized Version to be precise), nearly twenty times the length of this book.

When you look at the complete list of Bible books, getting to know the Bible seems daunting. You may never have heard of some of the books, let alone know what is in them. Coming across titles like Leviticus and Lamentations, Habakkuk and Hebrews is enough to make one's head spin! But don't worry, with a little patience everything will soon start falling into place.

Think of the Bible as a jigsaw. In chapter 4 we'll look at the big picture, like the one you see on the lid of a jigsaw box, but for now we will be content with examining a few of the pieces. It will give some idea of the colours and shapes we're working with.

Activity 1
Take a Bible, one with both Old and New Testaments, and turn to page 50. It will be a left-hand page round about the end of

Genesis or the beginning of Exodus. Read the first paragraph you come to on the page. Simply notice what kind of writing it is. It will probably be narrative – part of a story.

Turn on to page 100 and do the same. Then page 150, and so on throughout the whole Bible. At each stop, note the title of the book you're reading and something about the kind of writing. Is it prose or poetry? (Most Bibles indicate poetry with indented lines.) Is it narrative? Or legislation giving commands? Is it prayer or does it express worship? Is it philosophy or prophecy? Is it part of a letter giving advice or instruction? See how many different kinds of writing you can find.

By the time you get to the end, you'll have dipped into around two dozen Bible passages. Don't worry if you haven't understood much: the same would happen if you tried to read any book in such a random way. The important thing is to have glimpsed something of the wide range of writing styles found in the Bible. Through all of them God speaks today.

Activity 2

For this second activity, you'll need to find and read passages I have chosen for you. They go in order through the Bible and give a more systematic sampling of the different kinds of writing you've just met. I've chosen a fair and balanced selection, but not just easy passages. Read each one carefully; see what you make of it, but don't worry if you don't understand it all. Once you've given each passage some thought, go on to read my comments about it: these will give a few pointers as to where each passage fits in the overall jigsaw. There are sixteen selections, mostly complete chapters: I suggest you spread your reading over several days, taking one or two passages at a time.

Selection 1: Genesis 3: the Garden of Eden
This story – the Fall – comes immediately after the twin accounts of creation found in Genesis chapters 1 and 2. Tempted by the devil and disobeying God, Adam and Eve eat the

forbidden fruit. Notice the Bible never says it was an apple! The results are dire:

- Adam and Eve hide from God: the relationship with him is broken.

- They experience shame and guilt.

- Adam blames Eve, Eve blames the snake and – as one wit has put it – the snake doesn't have a leg to stand on!

- Pleasurable work becomes arduous toil.

- Adam and Eve are banished from Eden; access to eternal life is barred.

Some take this story literally; others are happy to accept it as figurative or symbolic. Either way, it describes the entrance of sin into the world and the resulting rift between humankind and God the Creator. With the coming of sin, spiritual death sets in to the human race.

Selection 2: Genesis 40: Joseph and the dreamers
The chapter opens with Joseph, the favourite of Jacob's twelve children, in prison in Egypt. Earlier chapters tell us how he got there and about his 'coat of many colours'. Resented for his dreams by his brothers, he was sold by them into slavery. In Egypt he became a trusted servant to Potiphar, a royal official who worked for Pharaoh, Egypt's king. But accused of attempted rape by Potiphar's lustful wife, he is thrown into prison and left to rot.

Sharing Joseph's cell are two disgraced palace officials, Pharaoh's cupbearer and baker. Both have a dream which Joseph interprets. The cupbearer gets out alive; the baker loses his head. But the next chapter reveals it is two whole years before the cupbearer remembers to put in a good word for Joseph.

Selection 3: Deuteronomy 5: God's Ten Commandments

Still in Egypt 400 years later, Joseph's descendants become Pharaoh's slaves. God calls Moses to lead them to freedom. Escaping, they spend forty years wandering in the desert before returning home to Canaan. The Book of Deuteronomy contains a series of speeches given by Moses to the people of Israel at the end of these desert wanderings. Most of the book is taken up with a restatement of the laws God gave at Mount Sinai at the beginning of their desert trek.

This chapter contains the Ten Commandments, the most important of all the laws God has given. The first four are about loving God; the last six about loving others. For comparison, notice how Jesus summarises them in Matthew 22:35–40.

Selection 4: Judges 4: assault with a deadly tent peg

Made into a film, some parts of the Bible would rate an 18-certificate! This is one of them. Now back in Canaan, the Israelites are led by a succession of military leaders known as judges. Deborah was one. This chapter describes a battle between Barak, commander of Deborah's army, and Sisera, commander of the enemy army.

Exhausted from the fighting, the defeated Sisera is lured into the tent of a woman called Jael. Thinking he is safe, he falls asleep. While he sleeps, she reaches for a tent peg: Sisera never knew what hit him!

Judges 5 records Deborah's victory song. It is one of the oldest pieces of poetry in the Bible. Jael's actions are praised in Judges 5:24–27.

Selection 5: 2 Samuel 11: King David's affair with Bathsheba

After the judges, Israel becomes a monarchy – ruled by kings. David is later described as 'a man after God's own heart' (Acts 13:22), but he also had serious failings. Second Samuel 11 describes his adultery with Bathsheba, a woman married to Uriah, a soldier. When Bathsheba falls pregnant, David arranges Uriah's death. How many of the Ten Commandments did David break? At least four!

The next chapter records how Nathan the prophet brought David back to his senses and helped him realise his serious wrongdoings.

Selection 6: Psalm 51: David's confession to God

David, a skilled musician, composed many of the psalms. Some, such as this, are linked to incidents in his life. Psalm 51 records his deep sorrow for his adultery which he now recognises as sin against God himself. The mention in verse 7 to being cleansed with hyssop is a reference to the practice of using a hyssop sprig to sprinkle animal blood around the altar to obtain God's forgiveness (see Heb 9:19).

Selection 7: Proverbs 1: listening to wisdom

The Book of Proverbs – mostly a collection of wise but pithy sayings – is introduced as 'the proverbs of Solomon son of David, king of Israel'. Verses 1–7 tell us the benefits of paying attention to these proverbs. More than anything else, they give wisdom. The rest of the chapter, in the form of fatherly advice, encourages us to do all we can to listen to wisdom and not to the voice of the morally foolish.

Selection 8: Ecclesiastes 3: a time for everything

Ecclesiastes is a depressing, pessimistic book. It describes the emptiness and futility of life. There is nothing new under the sun (1:9). If you recognise the opening words of chapter 3, it's probably because they were made famous in Pete Seeger's lyrics of the 1960s' folk song, 'Turn, turn, turn', sung by The Byrds. The writer of Ecclesiastes goes on to say everyone comes to the same inevitable end – death. Yet, earthbound though we are, God has 'set eternity in the hearts of men' (3:11).

Selection 9: Isaiah 9:1–7: a child is born

Isaiah is the first of the *major* prophets, so called because of their length. This passage, often read at Christmas, speaks of a light shining in the darkness. This light will come from Galilee (northern Israel) and will be in the form of a child upon whose shoulders will rest the government of God (v 6). This passage is messianic, ie it looks forward to the coming Messiah. Notice the four double titles given to the Messiah in verse 6, and remember that Isaiah uttered these words more than 700 years before Jesus was born!

Selection 10: Haggai 1: 'Get that temple built!'

Haggai is one of the *minor* – or shorter – prophets, tucked away towards the end of the Old Testament. It only has two chapters, so you may need to consult your Bible's contents page even to find it! The temple has been destroyed and the people exiled. As they return to Jerusalem seventy years later, Haggai encourages them and their leaders (principally the governor Zerubbabel and the high priest Joshua) to build a new temple for the Lord.

In chapter 4, you will get more of an idea where prophets like Isaiah and Haggai fit into the overall jigsaw. And chapter 7 considers each Old Testament prophetic book in turn.

Selection 11: Matthew 7: building on Jesus' words

We are now in the New Testament, the time of Jesus. Matthew chapters 5–7 contain the Sermon on the Mount (see 5:1). If your Bible has section headings, you'll see that this chapter covers a range of topics: not judging others (vs 1–6); effective prayer (vs 7–12); a choice of ways in life (vs 13,14); and true discipleship (vs 15–23). The last part, a parable about two builders, one wise and one foolish (vs 24–29), is a fitting conclusion to the whole sermon. Only if we build our lives on Jesus' teaching will they rest on a secure foundation.

Selection 12: Mark 15: Jesus' trial and death

Having run into conflict with the authorities, Jesus is betrayed and arrested. Mark 15 describes his trial before the Roman governor Pontius Pilate, his treatment at the hands of the Roman soldiers, his death by crucifixion and his burial in the borrowed tomb of Joseph from Arimathea. A graphic portrayal of Maundy Thursday and Good Friday.

Selection 13: Acts 16:11–40: Paul in prison at Philippi

After his resurrection, the Good News of Jesus spread like wildfire. No one did more to proclaim the Gospel and to establish the Christian Church than Paul, a converted Jew. On one missionary journey, he came to the Roman colony of Philippi.

The passage tells how he and his travelling companion Silas were imprisoned and the even more remarkable story of how they escaped. Paul lets on he is a citizen of Rome (a status that carried privilege) and receives an apology for his rough treatment. There were no church buildings then: the Christians met in the home of Lydia, a businesswoman and one of the first Christian converts in Philippi.

Paul later wrote a letter to this church – the letter to the Philippians – which we look at next.

Selection 14: Philippians 2:1–18: following the example of Christ

Again in prison for his faith, Paul wrote this letter to the believers at Philippi, perhaps ten or twelve years after first evangelising them. It is a warm letter, full of joy. In chapter 2, he urges his readers to be united and to follow Christ's humble example in serving one another.

Verses 6–11 form a wonderful statement of faith, a hymn of praise. They describe Jesus' stooping in obedient humility, followed by his exaltation to glory. Read them carefully and offer thanks to God.

Selection 15: 1 John 1:1 – 2:2: Jesus, God's answer for sin

Paul was not the only one to write letters to churches. John, one of Jesus' first disciples, did so too. (Don't confuse First John with John's Gospel.) Notice how in these verses the author describes himself as an eye-witness to the earthly life of Christ. He calls upon his readers to live in the light of Christ, to be honest about any sin in their lives, but also to rejoice in God's provision for forgiveness.

The idea of 'atoning sacrifice' in 2:2 recalls the Old Testament system of animal sacrifices. A perfect and willing sacrifice, Jesus died in our place and took upon himself the punishment that should have been ours.

The Bible was not originally written in chapters or verses: they were put in much later to help us find our way around. Sometimes, the Bible's chapter divisions are not in sensible places. Reading chapter 1 without the first two verses of chapter 2 does not make much sense, leaving us without knowing how our sins can be forgiven.

Selection 16: Revelation 21: heaven, here we come!

We began in the early chapters of Genesis; now we are in the Bible's closing verses. The Book of Revelation is a book of apocalyptic prophecy (see chapter 8 for more details). It is full of visions that are hard to interpret: many of them contain imagery from the Old Testament. But Revelation 21 is a wonderful picture. Heaven, the believer's future destiny, is compared with a new Jerusalem, perfect in every dimension. A temple is not needed because God is its glory. Its doors will always be open – but only to those whose names are in the Book of Life.

Some symbolism may need explaining:

- The Lamb (vs 22,23,27) is Jesus, God's sacrifice for sin;
- Alpha and Omega (v 6) are the first and final letters of the

Greek alphabet.

If you have read all sixteen passages, congratulations! It's a great start! You have done something really worthwhile: you've been reading the Bible for yourself, including bits some Christians find hard or never get around to. You may not have understood all you've read, but you've had a taste of the different kinds of writing the Bible contains and you've begun to see something of the big picture. We will explore more of that big picture in chapter 4, but first some suggestions on gaining a greater familiarity with your Bible.

3

Getting familiar: first approaches to Bible reading

INTRODUCTIONS have been made and first impressions formed. The Bible, a library of living books, lies before us. Just as it takes time to get to know a person well, it takes time and effort to gain familiarity with the Bible. This can be done alone or in the company of others.

Only since the advent of universal education in the nineteenth century has it been possible for most people to read the Bible for themselves. Before then, the only way for many to become acquainted with God's Word was to hear it read in the churches. When the Great Bible of 1539, a forerunner of the Authorized (King James) Version was placed in English churches, it was chained to the lectern to prevent people taking it away. A common sight was to see parishioners gathered round while anyone capable of doing so read aloud from it. This even took place during the less interesting parts of some church services! 'This is the Bible appointed to the use of the churches,' said the preface, an injunction similar to the one still found on the frontispiece of the Authorized Version of 1611, the eventual successor to the Great Bible.

The Bible belongs to the Church. It is the Church that has preserved, copied and translated the Old and New Testament Scriptures. Reading the Bible in private is like listening to music on your personal hi-fi; reading it with other Christians is like attending a live concert. Much more interesting and rewarding. But we have hi-fi systems because we cannot go to live concerts all the time.

Hearing, reading and studying the Bible alongside others is an invaluable means of growing as a Christian, but we can do that only once or twice a week. We need to feed on God's Word every day, not just Sundays! In this chapter, we'll look at how we can get more from our Bibles both at church and at home.

At church

At church we feed on God's Word in two ways: as receptive listeners and as active participants.

As receptive listeners

In almost every act of Christian worship the Bible is read aloud. One, two or even three Scripture readings may be included in a church service. Some churches follow a lectionary giving set readings Sunday by Sunday. Over a period of two or three years, much of the Bible is covered. Other churches use the Bible passages chosen by the preacher in readiness for his or her sermon.

The public reading of Scripture is an important element of worship. A gifted and well-rehearsed reader can bring the Bible to life if it is read with conviction, dignity, passion and with careful attention to the meaning of the text, as Ezra did in Old Testament times (see Neh 8:8).

In addition to the principal readings, other Bible verses may find their way into worship. Certain passages, the psalms for example, may be taken up into the liturgy of the church. And nearly all denominations use Paul's words from 1 Corinthians 11:23–26 to introduce the Service of Holy Communion.

Some churches provide a pew Bible. This gives everyone access to the same translation and makes it possible for the preacher to give page numbers to help the congregation locate a passage. Nevertheless, taking your own Bible to church is a good habit to fall into.

Some churches encourage the congregation to follow the Bible reading in the pew Bible. Evidence actually suggests more is taken in if the congregation keep their Bibles shut and listen attentively. The time to open your Bible is not during the reading, but in the sermon while the preacher expounds its meaning.

This is not the place to discuss the quality of contemporary preaching, but the preacher's job is to build a bridge between the world of the Bible and the world of today. He or she should be explaining, illustrating and applying its truth. The authority of preaching rests on the authority of Scripture. Take every opportunity to hear good preaching that opens up the Word of God.

As active participants

Nowadays many churches run small groups that meet informally, usually on a weekday evening. These groups have a variety of names and aims. Prayer and an opportunity to share news will often feature, but a central activity will be Bible study. Alongside other groups for more mature believers, some churches offer nurture groups designed for new Christians.

It is an excellent idea to belong to a Bible-study group. It is the best possible way to get into the Bible. Newcomers sometimes worry about answering a question wrongly or having nothing to contribute. There is no need to be anxious. Never be afraid to say you don't understand something or can't find the right passage; and never worry about asking a question, however basic it may seem. If the group is doing its job, it will be sensitive to your needs.

A little advance preparation can be helpful. It should be possible to find out beforehand what Bible passages are going to be studied. If possible, try to read at least the principal passage before attending the meeting.

Do your best to join a small group Bible study and attend regularly, taking your Bible with you. Make it a priority in your week.

At home

A little and often is a good adage when it comes to physical exercise or practising a musical instrument. The same is true when it comes to reading and studying the Bible at home. I wholeheartedly endorse and encourage a daily quiet time – the practice of reading a portion of the Bible, reflecting on it, and linking this to time spent with God in praise and prayer.

Married couples and Christian families may find a shared devotional time valuable, but it is also as important to spend time alone with God away from anybody else (see Matt 6:6). Bible reading and prayer go together naturally. Through the Bible God speaks to us; in prayer we speak to him. Space doesn't allow me to say more about prayer (though I've suggested some worthwhile books at the end of chapter 9), but I do want to say something about daily reading notes and to recommend their use before we look at other ways you can become more familiar with your Bible.

Bible reading notes

A wide range of daily reading notes is available to suit varying tastes and levels of spiritual growth. A list of publishers is given in chapter 9. Typically, a set of notes provides dated readings for two, three or four months. As well as offering comments on a Bible portion, the most helpful feature about reading notes is that they assign a passage to be read each day and thus help considerably with the discipline of maintaining a regular quiet time.

Some notes are *thematic*: they follow a topic across various passages from different parts of the Bible. Others are *systematic*: they work through a Bible book passage by passage. Some aim to cover the whole Bible over a given period. For instance, *Daily Bread*, Scripture Union's most popular title, cycles through the Bible every four years (see the Reading Plan at the end of this chapter).

Whatever kind of notes are adopted, a Bible passage will be

given: anything from a few verses to a whole chapter. *It is the Bible passage, not the notes, that is the more important.*

Scripture Union encourages a four-stage approach to spending time with God:

1. Prepare – come to God

Open your heart and life to receive God's Word. Prepare to listen to God's voice. Take time to become quiet and still in his presence. Confess any sins of which you are aware. Ask the Holy Spirit to help you understand God's Word and to respond to what he might show you.

2. Read

Read the Bible passage given, taking time to get the feel of it. You may need to read the passage – or parts of it – more than once. Reading aloud helps concentration and understanding. Begin to listen to what God is saying to you.

3. Explore

Explore the meaning of the Bible passage more deeply for yourself. Do this before you read the notes. The following, or similar, questions may help:

What is the main point being made in this passage?

(a) What do I learn about God? The Church? The world? Human nature? Myself?

(b) Is there a promise to claim, a command to obey, a warning to avoid or an example to copy?

(c) What is God saying? About me? My attitudes? My behaviour? My circumstances? My priorities? My relationships?

Only *after* you have begun to explore the passage for yourself should you turn to the notes. They will add to your understanding and perhaps suggest how you could make a response. There may be suggestions for prayer, for further reading or for action. After a while, you're quite likely to see truths in the passage that the writer of the notes fails to mention. God's Word is living and its truth inexhaustible. The writer of the notes has space to develop only one or two ideas: God's Spirit is not so limited!

4. Respond

Turn your discoveries about God into worship; your discoveries about the world and human nature into prayer; and your discoveries about yourself into a fresh resolve to follow God's call. Decide how to share these discoveries with others in word and action.

Finally, there will be other prayer needs, your own and those of other people, that you will want to bring to God. End with thanksgiving.

Reading the Bible in this way employs both mind and heart. Because it is so important we shall consider a worked example here. It is the first of our eight approaches to Bible reading: two more will be given in this chapter, the remainder in chapters 5 and 6.

Approach 1: quiet time reading

Our example of quiet time reading is from Luke 15:11–32. Find it in your Bible. Now we shall follow the four steps outlined above.

1. Prepare

Pray: ask the Holy Spirit to help you understand this parable and to respond appropriately.

2. Read

Read the passage two or three times, taking time to get the feel of it. We can see immediately that we are dealing with a parable. Parables usually have one main thrust.

At this stage we are asking the question: What does it *say*? As well as getting the thread of the story, we may find some cultural elements in the passage are alien to us as modern readers. Let's deal with these first:

- A father's property was normally inherited by his sons on his death. However, a father sometimes made over his property before death, on the understanding that the inheriting son would manage the estate for his ageing father's benefit. Normally, the oldest male child took legal precedence in inheritance rights.

- Two sorts of people were found in a typical household: children and slaves. To the casual observer, a well-treated slave might be mistaken for a son; but while a son had a permanent position within the family, a slave lacked this right (see John 8:35). Sandals (v 22) were a symbol of sonship; slaves went barefoot.

- Pigs were 'unclean' to Jews. Feeding pigs was the ultimate indignity.

- The robe and ring (v 22) were symbols of reinstatement and acceptance.

- A fattened calf (v 23) was an animal kept for special family festivities.

A study Bible, commentary or daily reading notes will give this kind of information.

3. Explore
Now we ask a deeper question: What does it *mean*? We will use the same questions as suggested above. I'll be more detailed than you might find possible at first.

1. What is the main point in this passage?
To grasp this, we need to see the passage in context. Often, only verses 11–24 – the part about the younger brother – are read.

But this cuts the parable off halfway through. Verses 25–32, covering the older brother's response, are equally important. And by reading the preceding verses (1–10), we discover the parable's true setting.

Luke 15:1,2 reveals why Jesus was telling this story. He was proving popular among tax-collectors and 'sinners'. But the religious types – the Pharisees and scribes – objected to Jesus associating with such riff-raff.

Another clue to understanding this story comes in verse 3: 'Jesus told them this *parable*.' Notice that 'parable' is singular. What follows are three connected stories – the lost sheep, the lost coin and the two sons. Three stories – one parable – all making the same main point. God's love, says Jesus, seeks the lost and rejoices when they are found.

The two preparatory short stories are like film trailers, readying us for the main feature. They underpin the central point Jesus is making – God's patient, searching love and heaven's joy at the safe return of a lost individual. However, the sheep (vs 3–7) is lost far from home, while the coin (vs 8–10) is lost at home. To me, this suggests that it is not only the younger son who is lost, but his older brother too – though in a different sense. The younger son is like the undesirables listening to Jesus. They are far from God, but there is a way back. God's love doesn't give up, but watches and waits, ready to embrace the repentant. No one is too bad; no one is beyond redemption.

His older brother has also put up a barrier against his father's love, but in a different way. Notice his resentment when his younger brother returns: he disowns him, calling him 'this son of yours' (v 30). And to his father he says (v 29): 'All these years I've been *slaving* for you.' The older brother saw himself as a slave, not a son. He thought he had to earn acceptance by his efforts, whereas in reality his father loved and accepted him because he was a son, a permanent family member (compare Rom 8:15–17).

Like the tut-tutting scribes and Pharisees when they saw

Jesus welcoming 'sinners', the older brother is sour and bitter. Now we see the full point of the story: Jesus is warning the religious types they are 'lost'. If they want to be God's children, it must be on the basis of God's undeserved love, not their religious efforts.

Jesus, a master story-teller, leaves the parable with no ending. Did the older brother join the feast or stay outside? We don't know. Jesus was inviting the scribes and Pharisees listening on the back row to supply their own ending. How would they respond to God's generous and overflowing love? And would they rejoice that 'sinners' and other unlikely candidates were being drawn into God's kingdom?

⊰⊱

I have spent more time on these exploratory questions than you might. But that is deliberate: can you see how just by carefully reading the text in front of you, a whole vista of meaning can open up? And I've also been dropping clues to the principles of Bible interpretation, a subject to which we'll return in chapter 5.

We'll be briefer with the remaining questions:

2. What do I learn about God? The church? The world? Human nature? Myself?

We learn a very great deal about God and his love. It searches; it waits; it takes the initiative to find the lost. And while we don't learn much here about the church or the world, we glean a lot about human nature. The younger son's pride had to be broken before he could return. And it was the pride of the older brother that kept him outside the celebrations.

3. Is there a promise, a command, a warning or example to note?

There is the promise that God's love will always welcome the truly sorry sinner, but chiefly this parable serves as a warning against spiritual pride. How does our pride come between us and God? And how does it put up a barrier to others as well as ourselves receiving the Gospel?

4. What is God saying to me?

Do you see yourself as more like the younger or older brother? If you feel far from God, be assured there is nothing you've done that God can't or won't forgive. You can return to him right now. Or perhaps you're like the older brother, seeking God's approval by your efforts rather than rejoicing in the security of his fatherly love. You can thank God that his love is unconditional and freely given.

4. Respond

These discoveries lead very naturally to praise and prayer. As well as praying through and acting upon any application we see directed at ourselves, we can use the parable as a starting point of praying for others. Personally, I find this parable a great encouragement in praying for non-Christian friends and family members. Who knows? Something may happen tomorrow to bring them to their senses (v 17), make them aware of their spiritual need and start them on a journey back towards God's loving and welcoming arms.

❧

In this basic quiet time approach to the Bible, we've been using both heart and mind. Using our minds, we have found out a lot simply by reading what's on the page in front of us. And by opening our hearts, hopefully God has spoken to us about his love and our response to it. Head and heart should never be divorced from each other. There is an element of *study* and an element of *reflection*. Both lead to response and application.

Hearing God's voice through his Word cannot be rushed; it takes time. We are not looking for anything deeply profound or of startling, earth-shattering significance: God's Word to us is often simple, straightforward and down-to-earth.

Why not go back over this passage for yourself. Don't worry if you don't see all the points I spotted. That's not the issue. In fact, you may well see points in this parable I've missed. But your situation and your experience of life are different from mine. Let God speak to you in your circumstances. Now we shall turn to two more approaches to Bible reading.

Approach 2: Chunk reading

In my first week at Bible college, there was one lecture I was anticipating with particular delight: 'Old Testament overview'. The Principal promised to take us through the Old Testament at the rate of a book a week. 'Great,' I thought, 'now I can grasp what these books are about.' In the very first lecture, she asked for a show of hands. Who, she wanted to know, had read Genesis before coming along. None had. Crossly, she informed us we had to read both Genesis *and* Exodus for the following week, otherwise no lecture. I took the point: if we want to know what's in the Bible, there is no substitute for actually reading it for ourselves. Relying on the summaries of others is insufficient.

Daily notes, sermons, group studies – all these provide ideal ways of homing in on just a few verses at a time. But we also need to stand back and look for the big picture. A connoisseur, examining a great work of art, will do two things. He will get in close and examine the detail, right down to individual brush-strokes. But he will also stand back and admire the whole. Scientists work the same way. Some look through microscopes at very small structures; others peer through telescopes at vast expanses of the cosmos. One without the other, the close-up without the big view, leaves an incomplete picture. The Bible is just the same.

In addition to the reading plans already mentioned, there are reading schemes and special editions of the Bible available to help you read through the entire Bible in one or two years. To do this takes real discipline and devotion and requires tackling anything up to five chapters a day. An alternative I prefer is 'chunk reading' – sitting down occasionally to read a whole Bible book in one go. This way it is possible to see the outline and contents of an entire book and eventually the sweep of the whole Bible, revealing as it does the grand design of God's plan of salvation for humankind.

Let's suppose your daily notes are taking you through Paul's letter to the Philippians, or that you are studying this letter over a period of several weeks with others in a home group, or that a series of sermons is being preached on it at church. A great idea would be to read right through Philippians in one sitting. What seems to be its main sections? The main ideas? Its overall tone? You won't take in all the detail – that's not the point – but you will be building up the big picture. And when you come to look in closer detail at particular sections, you'll see how they fit into the whole. You won't miss the wood for the trees.

Today we spend our time dissecting and analysing Scripture. There is value in this, but that was not how the writers imagined we would read what they had to say. When a letter from Paul, like Philippians, arrived at its destination, it would very likely be read in its entirety to the gathered congregation. Only later would it be analysed in closer detail. An overview of Philippians is given in chapter 8.

Sometimes the main point God may want to get across to us may not be visible when reading just shorter sections. For example, the Old Testament story of Joseph covers several chapters: Genesis 37–50. In chopping the story into short lengths, it is difficult to get that much out of each individual episode in Joseph's life. But the story begins to speak to us very powerfully when we take it as a whole. What we see is God taking a brash, arrogant youngster, bringing him down a peg or two, then raising him up for his divine purposes. But we see this only when we take the story in its entirety rather than piecemeal.

The Gospels have a special impact when read at one sitting. Many Christians only ever read little bits of the gospels here and there and never sit down to read any one of the four from start to finish. Those who have done so, reading Matthew or Mark, Luke or John straight through, invariably report what an impression it has made on them, revealing a picture of Jesus they've never seen before. My personal practice is to read one of the Gospels right through each year during Lent, the seven-week period running up to Easter, thus cycling through them all over a four-year period. The reading plan given at the end of this chapter is based on this practice.

A further reason for reading in chunks is the fact that some parts of the Bible, especially some Old Testament books, are rarely preached on in church or studied in small groups. Take Isaiah for instance. While passages such as the Christmas prophecies in chapters 9 and 11 or the Good Friday reading in chapter 53 may get a look in, little thought is ever given to the rest of the book and its historical setting. Parts of it are not easy to understand, it's true, but without them it would be like having a jigsaw in which some pieces are allowed to fall down the back of the sofa and become irretrievably lost, leaving the overall picture spoiled and incomplete.

If you want to have a go at chunk reading, the best place to start would be with one of the gospels. Mark is the shortest and easiest, taking about two hours to read. After that, try a short New Testament letter: Philippians, Colossians or James. Next on the list might be a bit of history from the Old Testament: the life of Abraham in Genesis, Moses in Exodus or David in Samuel and Kings. The books of Ruth and Jonah are exciting to read and quite short. Back to the New Testament and Acts – the story of the early church – is a good choice. And in the Old Testament, why not dip into the psalms? Chapter 7 suggests some you might pick.

Approach 3: Scripture memorisation

As our third approach to Bible reading, I want to commend the practice of memorising scripture. It is not as popular as it once was, but I believe it to be thoroughly worthwhile. We want to get into the Bible but learning Bible verses does more: it gets the Bible into us.

Memorising scripture is more than a mental activity; it is a spiritual exercise. But why do it at all? There are four reasons:

- God's Word will be planted in us. It can then take root, shaping our thinking and informing our behaviour.

- We can have verses at the ready for unexpected opportunities of witness.

- The Spirit can bring back a verse to the front of our minds when we need it, for example when we are facing temptation. Jesus used Scripture as his defence against spiritual attack (see Matt 4:1–11; Luke 4:1–13; compare Eph 6:17; Ps 119:11), but he certainly didn't have a Bible with him!

- We can bring a verse out of memory and meditate upon it while performing some mundane task.

How to memorise scripture:

- Choose the verse or verses you wish to memorise. It might simply be a verse that has struck you personally; it might be one that's useful in witnessing or counselling when you don't want to be fumbling around in a Bible; or it might be a series of key verses to help you remember your way around a particular Bible book.

- Read the verse in your Bible. Note its context. Perhaps underline it.

- Write it down on a card. Recite it aloud several times, including the reference. Use the process: READ → COVER → RECITE → CHECK.

- Keep this up for a few days. Go over your memory verse a week later and again a week after that. Periodically revise all your verses.

Here are some verses you might like to commit to memory. They are all taken from Paul's letter to the Romans (all in the NIV), and between them they form a succinct summary of the Gospel message:

> I am not ashamed of the gospel, because it is the power of God for the salvation of everyone who believes (1:16).

> All have sinned and fall short of the glory of God (3:23).

> God demonstrates his own love for us in this: While we were still sinners, Christ died for us (5:8).

> The wages of sin is death, but the gift of God is eternal life in Christ Jesus our Lord (6:23).

> You did not receive a spirit that makes you a slave again to fear, but you received the Spirit of sonship. And by him we cry, 'Abba, Father.' The Spirit himself testifies with our spirit that we are God's children (8:15,16).

> We know that in all things God works for the good of those who love him, who have been called according to his purpose (8:28).

> We are more than conquerors through him who loved us (8:37).

> Therefore, I urge you, brothers and sisters, in view of God's mercy, to offer your bodies as living sacrifices, holy and pleasing to God – this is your spiritual act of worship. Do not conform any longer to the pattern of this world, but be transformed by the renewing of your mind. Then you will be able to test and approve what God's will is – his good, pleasing and perfect will (12:1,2).

Responding to Scripture

Finally, before we leave this chapter, I want to say a little more about the application of Scripture and our responses to God's Word.

We live in an individualistic world, a world which tends to dismiss anything that is not personally and immediately relevant. Often, the Bible will be personally and immediately relevant; if so, we should of course act upon what God is saying. But often there may not be an immediate or personal response. I like to think there are four ways in which we can respond to God's Word:

(a) Outward responses

This is when we see some action to take, something to do or stop doing, or some change that is called for in our behaviour or lifestyle. A sin to stop, a relationship to put right, a person to witness to, a career change to consider, a gift to make to a missionary agency are all examples.

If the appropriate response is outward, we should seek to act upon it without delay.

(b) Upward responses

More often, our response to God's Word will be God-directed: the offering of thanks or worship; confession and repentance of sin; an expression of trust, consecration or deeper commitment.

Let me make a personal plea at this point. When you turn to prayer, keep your Bible open. Before launching into a shopping list of requests, begin with reflection, thanksgiving or worship, appropriate to what you have just read.

The Bible itself can be used as a vehicle of praise and prayer. Do you feel your words are inadequate to express the greatness of God? Why not use the words of the Bible? Try Psalm 145 or 148 for size. The psalms are also an excellent source for prayer. Does God seem far away? Look at Psalm 42. Do you have a sin to confess? Psalm 103 might help express what you need to say, and through it you can receive the assurance of God's forgiveness.

And how do we pray for ourselves and our fellow Christians? So often, we pray that God will make our/their lives comfortable and our/their day run smoothly. Paul's prayer in Ephesians 3:16–19 suggests a better way of praying: for spiritual strength and for growth in our knowledge and love of God. When you pray, keep your Bible open. It is the best combined hymn book and prayer book there is!

(c) Inward responses

Reading and studying God's Word is about shaping our minds and thinking processes. Exposure to God's Word trains us to think the way God wants us to think; it helps us bring our lives into alignment with his purposes and will. God's Word counteracts worldly ways of thinking which constantly invade our minds. 'Don't let the world around you squeeze you into its own mould, but let God re-make you so that your whole attitude of mind is changed. Thus you will prove in practice that the will of God is good, acceptable to him and perfect (Rom 12:2, J. B. Phillips).

The effect of God's Word is accumulative in this respect. Eating plenty of fruit and vegetables for a day or even a week will make little immediate improvement to our health, but eating healthy food as a lifestyle choice will make a noticeable difference. God's Word is like that. Frankly, some parts of the Bible are more stirring than others. Sometimes we'll come across exciting truths, comparable with a slap-up gourmet meal, the words overflowing with rich meaning and deep relevance. But on other days it may seem like we're chewing through a bowl of bran. Humdrum perhaps, but still equally nutritious and part of the balanced nourishment we need. It was no accident that Jesus compared God's Word with our daily bread (Matt 4:4).

(d) Delayed response

Sometimes there is no immediate response we can make to God's Word. We might, for instance, be reading a psalm in which the writer cries out to God for help in time of trouble. If we're not facing difficulty ourselves, the psalm may not fit our mood, but what we can do is to tuck it away in the inner recesses of our mind and heart. The day will surely come when we do need it, when we can draw on its strength and wisdom.

> Let the word of Christ dwell in you richly as you teach and admonish one another with all wisdom, and as you sing psalms, hymns and spiritual songs with gratitude in your hearts to God. And whatever you do, whether in word or deed, do it all in the name of the Lord Jesus, giving thanks to God the Father through him (Col 3:16,17).

Appendix: Reading plan

The plan found below, based on the new four-year syllabus of Scripture Union's *Daily Bread* reading notes, covers most of the Bible. It is intended to be used for 'chunk reading' as described earlier in this chapter. One long book, or two short books, is a workable monthly target.

New Testament:

Year 1	Year 2	Year 3	Year 4
Mark	Luke	Matthew	John
Acts 1–8	Acts 9–14	Acts 15:1 – 21:16	Acts 21:17 – end
Hebrews Ephesians 1,2,3 John 1,2 Thess Jude	Romans Colossians James	1 Corinthians Philippians 1,2 Timothy Titus	2 Corinthians Galatians 1,2 Peter Philemon
			Revelation

Old Testament:

Year 1	Year 2	Year 3	Year 4
Genesis	Exodus	Numbers	Leviticus Deuteronomy
Joshua Judges Ruth	1 Samuel	2 Samuel 1 Kings	2 Kings Ezra Nehemiah Esther
Isaiah 1–39 Jonah Habakkuk	Isaiah 40–66 Joel Micah	Jeremiah Hosea Amos	Ezekiel Daniel Haggai Malachi
Job	Proverbs 1–10	Proverbs 11–31	Ecclesiastes Song of Songs
One psalm a week will get you through the Book of Psalms in four years			

Bible Timeline (1)

§1 <u>The Founders</u>

Adam & Eve

Cain & Abel

Noah

Abraham leaves
Ur for Canaan

2000 BC

§2 <u>The Ancestors</u>

Abraham

Isaac

Jacob

Joseph

Joseph settles
in Egypt

Jacob fathered the
12 tribes of Israel

§3 <u>The Slaves</u>

Population grows but
is enslaved in Egypt

§4 <u>The Wanderers</u>

Exodus from Egypt

Canaan conquered

Moses

The LAW
given

Joshua

§5 <u>The Judges</u>

Judges

Ruth

§6 <u>The Early Kings</u>

Samuel

Saul

1000 BC *Jerusalem made capital*

First Temple built

930 Kingdom divides

David

Solomon

Books of
POETRY
written

Bible Timeline (2)

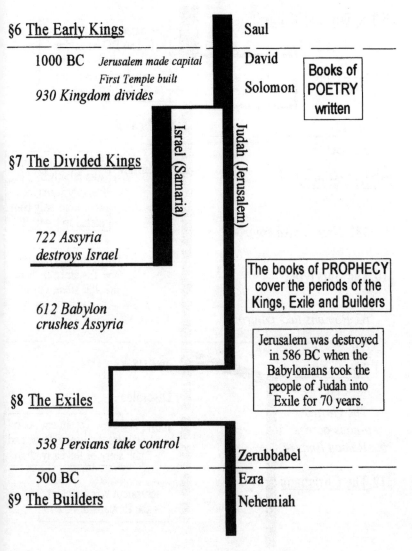

§6 <u>The Early Kings</u>

1000 BC *Jerusalem made capital*

First Temple built

930 *Kingdom divides*

§7 <u>The Divided Kings</u>

722 *Assyria destroys Israel*

612 *Babylon crushes Assyria*

§8 <u>The Exiles</u>

538 *Persians take control*

500 BC

§9 <u>The Builders</u>

Israel (Samaria)

Judah (Jerusalem)

Saul

David

Solomon

Zerubbabel

Ezra

Nehemiah

Books of POETRY written

The books of PROPHECY cover the periods of the Kings, Exile and Builders

Jerusalem was destroyed in 586 BC when the Babylonians took the people of Judah into Exile for 70 years.

Bible Timeline (3)

§7 <u>The Divided Kings</u>

§8 <u>The Exiles</u>

Jerusalem was destroyed
in 586 BC when the
Babylonians took the
people of Judah into
Exile for 70 years.

Zerubbabel

500 BC

Ezra

Nehemiah

§9 <u>The Builders</u>

Jerusalem's Temple
was rebuilt by 516.
The city walls, how-
ever, were only com-
pleted in c.440 BC.

332 Greeks take control

§10 <u>The Survivors</u>

Between the Old and
New Testaments, there
are 400 silent years.

63 Romans take control

AD 0

§11 <u>The Saviour</u>

JESUS

Disciples

*The Gospel
spreads across
the Roman Empire*

Paul

The New Testament period
covers the life of Jesus and
the story of the early church

§12 <u>The Christians</u>

Jerusalem was attacked
by the Romans in AD 70

4

The big picture

IMAGINE a traditional jigsaw picture: an English country cottage surrounded by a garden. One way to get started is to sort the pieces. There are pieces that make up the brickwork of the walls, the thatched roof, the door and windows, the flower garden, the lawn and, of course, the sky – where we have dozens of pieces that look almost identical.

We can think of the Bible as a 66-piece jigsaw. As we saw in chapter 1, it contains different kinds of writing: pieces of history, law, poetry, wisdom, prophecy, gospels, letters and more. The following diagram shows the major divisions of the Bible into its different kinds of writing:

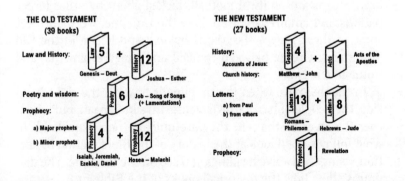

THE OLD TESTAMENT
(39 books)

Law and History: Law **5** + History **12**
Genesis – Deut   Joshua – Esther

Poetry and wisdom: Poetry **6** Job – Song of Songs
                                (+ Lamentations)
Prophecy:

a) Major prophets Prophecy **4** + Prophecy **12**
b) Minor prophets Isaiah, Jeremiah, Hosea – Malachi
                   Ezekiel, Daniel

THE NEW TESTAMENT
(27 books)

History:
Accounts of Jesus: Gospels **4** + Acts **1** Acts of the
Church history: Matthew – John   Apostles

Letters:
a) from Paul   Letters **13** + Letters **8**
b) from others Romans –   Hebrews – Jude
                Philemon

Prophecy: Prophecy **1** Revelation

It is now time to inspect the big picture: making sense of a jigsaw without access to the picture on the box lid is bad news. We'll start with the Bible's timeline – the historical thread running from beginning to end. In this chapter we will see how the twenty-two historical books (seventeen from the Old Testament; five from the New) fit together; in chapter 7 we will find out how the books of poetry and prophecy fit into the Old Testament; and in chapter 8 we will learn how the letters fit into the New Testament.

Understanding the timeline provides a sense of scale and a framework into which all the other pieces fit. It is like starting with the corner and edge pieces of a jigsaw, making it much easier to complete the rest. Many study Bibles include such a timeline, but we'll be using the one at the start of this chapter. Familiarise yourself with it now.

In all, the Bible covers some 2,000 years of history. Most of this is in the Old Testament. The New Testament covers a time span of under 100 years and in practice it concentrates on just a third of a century. Much of the Old Testament is concerned with Israel's efforts to keep its place in the land promised by God. This land goes under different names at different times – Canaan, Israel, Judah, Palestine, Judea – but they are all the same place. Though central to the Old Testament story, Israel was never a large or powerful nation. Only about the size of Wales, it has been a constant political football, kicked about by other larger nations and empires. As we follow the timeline, we shall meet some of these: Egypt, Assyria, Babylonia and Persia in the Old Testament; Greece between the Old and New Testaments; and Rome in the New.

In the diagram, when the timeline is towards the right-hand side, the people of Israel (the Israelites) are in Canaan; but whenever it moves to the left, they are outside their homeland. In what follows, we'll look at the history of the Bible section by section, using the twelve headings you see on the timeline. The diagrams show how the historical books of the Bible fit in.

§1. The founders

The Bible opens with a magnificent double account of creation (Gen 1,2) and other important stories that act as a prologue for all that is to follow. Whether one takes these stories literally or figuratively, they teach important truths about humankind's relationship to God, to the natural world and to other human beings.

God declares his original creation to be 'good' and 'very good' (Gen 1). Humankind is made in the image of God (Gen 1:26,27). But soon that image is marred by rebellious disobedience. The relationship between Creator and created is broken and the way to the tree of life barred (Gen 3). Sin against God leads to sin between brothers and neighbours (Gen 4). God appears to regret he ever made humankind, but one family – Noah's – is kept alive in an ark which floats across a flooded landscape (Gen 6–9). But soon – in the story of the Tower of Babel (Gen 11) – Noah's descendants are busy trying once again to prove that human beings can live without reference to God.

GENESIS 1-11

The stories of the Founders (to which no dates can realistically be given) occupy Genesis chapters 1–11.

> **Creation**
>
> **Adam & Eve**
>
> **Cain & Abel**
>
> **Noah's ark**
>
> **Babel: division of the nations**

§2. The ancestors

The story of Israel as God's chosen nation begins in earnest with a wandering herdsman called Abraham. God told Abraham (originally named Abram) and his wife Sarah (Sarai) to leave their home in southern Iraq ('Ur of the Chaldeans' in biblical parlance) and to journey, via Haran, to Canaan. A Bible atlas will show the route. Although the nomadic Abraham never made a permanent home in Canaan, God made him a double promise: that he would be 'the father of a great nation' dwelling in Canaan, and that 'other nations would be blessed' on account of him (Gen 12:1-3).

Abraham grew old but apart from Ishmael, born to Hagar his concubine, he remained childless. He wondered if God's promise would ever come true. But a son and legitimate heir – Isaac – was eventually born to Sarah and Abraham. Isaac, in turn, had a family – twin brothers, Esau and Jacob. Although Esau was the older, it was Jacob who obtained his father's blessing and thus became heir to God's promises. Jacob (renamed Israel) became the father of the twelve tribes of Israel (see Abraham's family tree in chapter 10). Jacob's favourite son was Joseph of technicolor dreamcoat fame. Scorned by his brothers, Joseph was sold into slavery and found himself in Egypt. Falsely

The stories of Abraham (c. 2000 BC) and the other ancestors fill the rest of Genesis, from chapter 12 to the end. Another Bible character who probably lived at the same time was Job (see under 'Poets' in chapter 7).

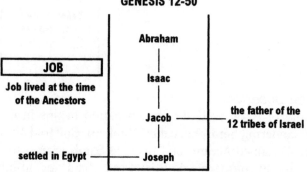

GENESIS 12-50

accused of attempted rape, he languished in prison for several years. But his talent for interpreting dreams enabled him to rise to power and help the Egyptian Pharaoh survive a seven-year famine.

This same famine forced Joseph's brothers, together with their father Jacob, to leave Canaan and migrate to Egypt. Reconciled to Joseph, the entire group settled permanently in Egypt and were to remain there for more than four centuries.

§3. The slaves

When Jacob moved with his family to Egypt, it was a small group of just a few dozen (Exodus 1:5, Acts 7:14). Between the end of Genesis and the start of the next Bible book, Exodus, we jump 400 years: there are a few holes in our jigsaw! Two important things happen in this period. First, there is a population explosion. The Israelites, descendants of Jacob, greatly increase in number. Second, threatened by this growth in the foreign population living among them, the Egyptians force the Israelites into slavery. This is how the Book of Exodus begins and it sets the scene for one of the most important events in the Bible – the exodus – meaning exit or escape.

Towering over the pages of this period is the figure of Moses. At the time Moses was born, Pharaoh had decreed that all male Israelite infants should be drowned in the Nile. Moses' mother put her newborn in a basket in the reeds by the Nile. He was pulled out of the water and adopted by Pharaoh's daughter. Although raised as an Egyptian, Moses never forgot his Hebrew roots. Having fled Egypt, Moses' attention was caught by God through means of a burning bush in the desert (Exod 3). God called Moses to challenge Pharaoh and to lead the enslaved Israelites to freedom.

Pharaoh was naturally reluctant to lose this source of cheap labour, but Moses demonstrated God's power through a series of ten devastating plagues (Exod 7–12). The last was the Passover (Exod 12): every firstborn of the Egyptians died, but

God's destroying angel 'passed over' the homes of the Israelites. The Israelites fled, making good their escape through the Red Sea,[1] through which God had miraculously created a dry patch. The exodus is one of the most significant events in Bible history and the rest of scripture often looks back to it. It is a picture of Christ's rescue of us from the slavery of sin. Some scholars date the Exodus around 1450 BC; others put it later – about 1280 to 1260 BC.

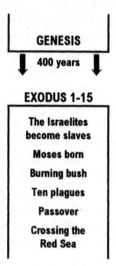

Moses' early life and the events leading up to the Red Sea crossing are told in Exodus 1-15.

GENESIS

400 years

EXODUS 1-15

The Israelites become slaves

Moses born

Burning bush

Ten plagues

Passover

Crossing the Red Sea

§4. The wanderers

The Israelites, having escaped Egypt, could have been back home in Canaan in a matter of weeks. But it became a trek of forty years. As soon as they left, the Israelites started grumbling. They moaned about the lack of food and water in the desert, and although God provided bread from heaven (called 'manna'), they continued to test his forbearance.

Three months after leaving Egypt, the Israelites came to Mount Sinai. Staying there a year, they were given God's law, including the Ten Commandments (Exod 20). God and his people entered into an agreement – or covenant. If they were faithful to him, blessing would follow; but if they were disobedient, they would lose their privileges – including the land promised to them – until such times as they repented and turned back to God.

Along with the moral law, the Israelites were given instructions about the sacrifices they were to perform, the special annual festivals they were to celebrate (see chapter 10 for details) and instructions on building a special tent, known as the 'Tent of Meeting' or 'Tabernacle'. This was a portable place of worship they carried with them through the desert and erected wherever they pitched camp. At the centre of the Tent was a special chest, the Ark of the Covenant, containing among other things the stone tablets on which the law was written. Sacrifices took place on an altar in the enclosure surrounding the Tent. These offerings were administered by priests chosen from the tribe of Levi, one of the twelve tribes descended from Jacob that formed the loose-knit infant nation of Israel. Aaron, Moses' brother, was the nation's first High Priest.

Despite these advantages, the Israelites tried God's patience. On one occasion, they melted gold into the shape of a calf and began to worship that instead of the Lord (Exod 32). On another, two years into their journey when they sent a scouting party over the border into Canaan, they concluded the country was too difficult to capture even with God's promised help (Numbers 13,14). As a result, God decided that the Israelites who left Egypt would not see Canaan, only their children. Almost an entire generation, including Moses himself, died in the desert. Of those who left Egypt, Caleb and Joshua were the only two to enter the promised land.

Four Bible books cover this forty-year period of history: Exodus (chapters 15–40), Leviticus, Numbers and Deuteronomy.

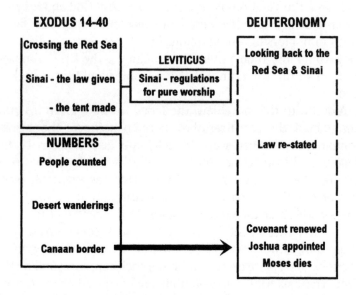

Chronologically, the Book of Numbers continues where Exodus ends and completes the account of the desert wanderings. The regulations found in Leviticus were given while Israel was at Sinai. Deuteronomy contains a series of sermons given by Moses at the end of the desert wanderings. These look back over the historical period covered by Exodus and Numbers, but central to Deuteronomy is a restatement of God's Law and the renewal of his covenant with the people of Israel.

There are different kinds of law found in these books:

- Moral laws – still applicable today, eg the Ten Commandments.

- Civil laws – necessary for a just and peaceful society. While these first applied to Israel's agricultural society of 3,500 years ago, many of the underlying principles are still relevant today.

- Ceremonial laws – regulations for worship, including sacrifices and offerings. These point to Christ's perfect sacrifice and the offering of himself upon the Cross. They remind us of God's holiness and our need of forgiveness.

- Cleanliness laws – laws about hygiene and ritual purity, distinguishing what is 'clean' and 'unclean'. Again, superseded by Christ.

Parts of these books, such as the details of the ceremonial and cleanliness laws in Leviticus and the measurements of the Tent in Exodus, are not essential reading for the new Christian. Rather like the pieces of sky in a jigsaw – difficult to fit in until the end – these bits are best left until other sections of the Bible have been tackled.

§5. The Judges

The next stage in the history of the Israelites begins when they cross the River Jordan – miraculously parted like the Red Sea had been – and establish a foothold in Canaan after an absence of more than four centuries (Joshua 3). Not surprisingly, the country had been occupied by others in the meantime. Under the leadership of Joshua, the first of many challenges to face the Israelites was the walled city of Jericho (Joshua 6).

It took time to conquer the land, but as they did so, it was shared out between the Israelite tribes. After the death of Joshua, there was no formal leadership, but a series of judges – or deliverers – were called by God as the need arose. A repeated and unhappy cycle of behaviour took place:

1 The people forget the Lord, often to worship other gods.

2 God allows an enemy to overrun the Israelites.

3 The Israelites call upon God for help.

4 God sends a judge/deliverer to save them.

5 Safe and smug again, the people forget God once more.

The judges were not like today's judges. Although they had a role in settling legal disputes, their main task was to provide military leadership. The first judge was Joshua and the last Samuel. The best known are Deborah, Gideon and Samson (see chapter 10 for a full list). The period of the judges lasted until c. 1050 BC when Israel's first king came to the throne. During the time of the judges, Israel remained a loose federation of tribes rather than a unified nation.

Samuel, Israel's last and greatest judge, was a wise and godly man. Under his leadership, Israel knew peace and spiritual strength. Samuel brought considerable unity to the nation, so much so that its people wanted a king as the surrounding nations already had. Although Samuel warned the people that a king would put their men in his army, their women in his harem and – worst of all – their taxes in his coffers, the people insisted on a king. Samuel appointed first Saul and later David as the first in a long line of kings.

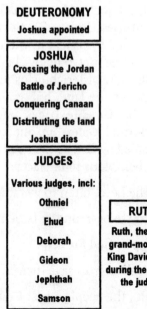

DEUTERONOMY
Joshua appointed

JOSHUA
Crossing the Jordan
Battle of Jericho
Conquering Canaan
Distributing the land
Joshua dies

JUDGES
Various judges, incl:
Othniel
Ehud
Deborah
Gideon
Jephthah
Samson

RUTH
Ruth, the great grand-mother of King David, lived during the time of the judges

§6. The Early Kings

The first three kings of Israel ruled a united nation. Their lives are told in considerable detail. In order they are Saul, David and Solomon. Each reigned for about forty years. David's reign can be conveniently dated to 1000 BC.

Saul was a disaster; he did not serve God faithfully. And he suffered from extreme paranoid tendencies. He employed David as giant-slayer, harp-player and, eventually, army commander. But David was too successful. Israelite women sang a song: 'Saul has slain his thousands, David his tens of thousands' (1 Sam 18:7). Saul's son Jonathan became David's closest friend and Michal, Saul's daughter, became his wife. This made Saul feel even more isolated. More than once Saul attempted to murder David. David fled from Saul but never took revenge. Much of Saul's energy was expended in trying to locate and kill David. Eventually Saul, along with Jonathan, died in battle. David mourned their deaths. David then became king.

David, despite such failures as his adultery with Bathsheba, is described as 'a man after God's own heart' (1 Sam 13:14; Acts 13:22). He was a great military leader: Israel's borders grew to their greatest extent under his reign. One of his most notable achievements was to capture Jerusalem (2 Sam 5), a city that had remained unconquered throughout the years of the judges. David made this fortified, hill-top citadel his capital. David also left a great spiritual legacy, composing many of the psalms.

David's son Solomon was the next king. He is known for three things: wisdom, wealth and women! The first was his strength; the last two his weaknesses! His finest achievement was to build Israel a temple (1 Kings 6 and 2 Chr 3), thus confirming Jerusalem as the nation's spiritual as well as military capital. Solomon, however, was half-hearted in his love of God. According to 1 Kings 11:3 he had 700 foreign wives and 300 concubines! He allowed these to worship their own gods – such as the Moabite god Chemosh and the Ammonite god Molech – and was himself drawn into worshipping such idols. In addition, he drained the wealth of the country in order to build the temple and his own much more lavish palace. Those taxes again! The result? The northern part of the country, distant from Jerusalem, grew restless. On Solomon's death, there was civil war. The country split in two.

The Bible books that cover this period are 1 & 2 Samuel and 1 Chronicles, together with the early parts of 1 Kings and 2 Chronicles. We'll see how they all fit together at the end of the next section which completes the period when God's people lived under a monarchy.

§7. The Divided Kings

When the country split on Solomon's death, it divided into north and south. Each had its own king. The north – Israel – had its capital first at Shechem, later at Samaria; the south – Judah – kept Jerusalem as its principal city.

Rehoboam, a son of Solomon, was put on the throne of the united nation. When asked if he would reduce the heavy burden of taxes from which the north benefited little, Rehoboam replied that he would demand more, not less (1 Kings 12:1-24). Civil war ensued. Jeroboam, a treacherous royal official, became king of Israel. The north-south divide took place in 930 BC and was never healed.

From this point on, the Bible pronounces a verdict on each king of Judah and of Israel. They are judged either as 'doing good in the eyes of the Lord' or as 'doing evil'. Of Judah's nineteen kings and one queen, a mere eight get the thumbs up. Two of the best were Hezekiah (2 Kings 18–20) and Josiah (2 Kings 22,23), both of whom brought spiritual renewal to Judah. Of Israel's twenty kings, all without exception get the thumbs down. The worst was Ahab (1 Kings 16–22), aided and abetted by his wife, Jezebel, who even today lends her name to shamelessness and notoriety.

Israel – the northern kingdom

Of the two nations, Israel was by far the larger and stronger, but its history was shorter – just 200 years. Lacking a central place of worship, Israel and her kings were more easily tempted into the worship of foreign gods. And being in closer proximity to their enemies, there was considerable political as well as spiritual compromise. In the time of Ahab for example, his Phoenician consort Jezebel cultivated the worship of her favourite god, Baal. The Israelite prophet Elijah denounced this and said God would withhold rain from Israel (1 Kings 17:1). And in a contest between him and 850 prophets of Baal and Asherah on Mount Carmel, Elijah called fire down from heaven to demonstrate the superior strength of the Lord (1 Kings 18). Another who spoke up against Israel's spiritual folly was Elijah's prophetic successor, Elisha.

But their voices, and the voices of other prophets such as Amos and Hosea, went unheeded. The end came in 722 BC when Assyria, the superpower of its day, crushed Israel. Its people were scattered, never to return, and the land repopulated by strangers. Israel's fall is recorded in 2 Kings 17.

Judah – the southern kingdom

Judah fared better than her northern counterpart – 350 years in all. For the first half century, there was near constant civil war with Israel. But soon Judah, like Israel, came under threat: first from Syria (Aram in some Bible translations) and then Assyria (the two should not be confused). Unlike Israel, Judah just survived the Assyrian onslaught. Judah's own nemesis came in the form of the Babylonians who, in 612 BC, took control of Nineveh, the former Assyrian capital, and continued to grow in power thereafter. Prophets to Judah during this period included Isaiah, Micah, Zephaniah, Habakkuk and Jeremiah. See Chapter 7.

With Babylonian power on the increase and a threat to everyone in the region, Pharaoh Neco of Egypt marched north towards the stronghold of Carchemish to take a stand against the Babylonian advance (2 Kings 23:29,30; 2 Chron 35:20–24). Unhappy with this, King Josiah of Judah marched to intercept Neco at Megiddo. Josiah was killed in battle and Judah came under Egyptian control. Josiah's spiritual reforms were brought to an end. The Egyptians placed Josiah's son Jehoiakim on the throne – a puppet king. When, in 605 BC, Neco's troops stationed at Carchemish were routed by the Babylonians (Jer 46:2), control of Judah passed into Babylonian hands.

In 597 BC, Judah made the mistake of rebelling against Babylonian rule. King Nebuchadnezzar of Babylon acted swiftly: he marched into Judah and besieged Jerusalem. Jehoiakim's son, Jehoiachin, took the throne but surrendered after only three months. Jerusalem was taken and the leading citizens of Judah were exiled to Babylon. Nebuchadnezzar made Zedekiah, Jehoiachin's uncle, into another puppet king. But he too rebelled against Nebuchadnezzar. The Babylonian army marched again and in 586 BC Jerusalem fell and its temple was destroyed. Even more were deported. Ethnic cleansing is nothing new.

The Bible asserts that the reason for the fall – first of Israel, then of Judah – was the faithlessness of the people and their rulers towards God. The covenant was broken, resulting in expulsion from the land God had given them (see for example Jer 16:10–13).

The period of the early and divided kings is covered by six Bible books: the two books each of Samuel, Kings and Chronicles (originally each was one volume). The books of Samuel and Kings run consecutively, but the two books of Chronicles run in parallel with the books of 2 Samuel and 1 and 2 kings, repeating much of what they say. The reign of one king, Hezekiah, is actually recorded in three places, in 2 Kings 18–20, 2 Chronicles 29–32 and Isaiah 36–39. This diagram will explain:

Some important differences between the books of Samuel/Kings and Chronicles should be noted:

- After a long list of names (chs 1-9) and a brief mention of

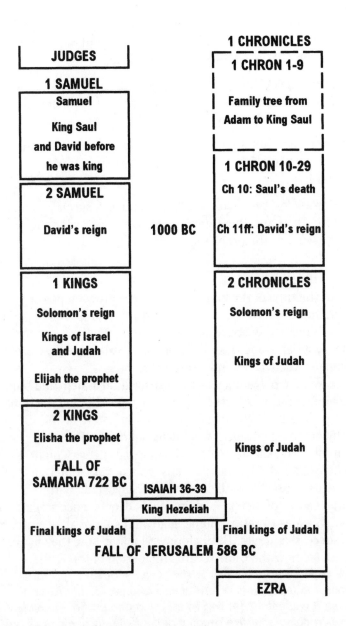

Saul's death (ch 10), 1 Chronicles begins with the life of King David. Only 1 Samuel gives any details about Samuel, Saul or the life of David before he became king.

- Chronicles paints generally rosy pictures of David, Solomon and some of the other kings; the books of Samuel and Kings tell their stories 'warts and all'.

- After the split in 930 BC, 2 Chronicles follows only the fortunes of Judah. Kings includes the histories of both Judah and Israel.

- Chronicles, more so than Kings, shows a special interest in Jerusalem and the Temple. Kings has a greater interest in the work of the prophets.

§8. The Exiles

From the time of the kings onwards, the growing power of surrounding nations plays an increasingly important part in Israel's history. We have already met the Egyptians, the Syrians, the Assyrians and the Babylonians. Still to come are the Persians, the Greeks and the Romans.

It was the Babylonians who destroyed Jerusalem and took its inhabitants into exile, the first group in 597 BC and the remainder in 586 BC. But only half a century later, in 538 BC, the Babylonians themselves were defeated by the Persians. Daniel, a prophet in exile, foretold and witnessed the very night it happened (Daniel 5). The Persians had a very different policy towards those the Babylonians had deported. Within a year, King Cyrus of Persia had issued a decree encouraging the Jewish exiles to return home. Many did so, not all at once, but in successive waves. But before we look at how they fared, we must see how the Bible records the period of the Exile.

The exile lasted some fifty to sixty years – or seventy years measured from the time Jerusalem's temple was destroyed to when it was rebuilt (586–516 BC). No one part of the Bible gives a comprehensive account of the Exile. Its beginnings are recorded at the very end of 2 Kings and 2 Chronicles and in the closing chapter of the prophet Jeremiah. The grief of the people when Jerusalem and its Temple were destroyed are poignantly portrayed in Lamentations.

Two prophets, Ezekiel and Daniel, delivered their messages during the exile (see chapter 7 for details). Daniel reveals how hard it was for the Jews to stand up for their faith. He was dropped into a pit of lions for praying to his God (Dan 6); and his three friends were thrown into a fiery furnace for not bowing down to a statue of Nebuchadnezzar (Dan 3).

Materially, conditions in exile were not too bad, but the Jews felt spiritually bereft away from Jerusalem and their temple. It was difficult for them to understand that God could be with them so far from home. Psalm 137, written in the Exile, expresses how they felt: By the rivers of Babylon we sat and wept when we remembered Zion [Jerusalem]. How can we sing the songs of the Lord while in a foreign land? (vs 1,4)

Another book relating to the Exile is Esther. Not all the Jews did return from Persia. Two who stayed were Mordecai and his beautiful young cousin Esther. Mordecai uncovered a plot to destroy all the Jews living in the Persian capital of Susa. Esther, risking her privileged position in the royal palace, was able to expose the plot and save her people. Her actions are still celebrated in the Jewish feast of Purim.

§9. The Builders

The exiles returned to Judah in at least three waves, following the decree issued by the Persian king Cyrus which allowed them to do so. The main party left Babylon in 538 BC. Under the leadership of two men, Zerubbabel (a descendant of the last king of Judah) and Joshua, the high priest (not to be confused with the much earlier Joshua, the first of the judges), this group laid the foundations for a new temple. However, opposition from foreign settlers (now populating what had been the northern kingdom of Israel), forced them to stop. Encouraged by two prophets, Haggai and Zechariah, the work re-started and the temple was eventually completed in 516 BC, some seventy years after the destruction of its predecessor.

Two further but later leaders were Ezra and Nehemiah. Not all scholars agree on dates, but the traditional view is that Ezra came to Jerusalem in 458 BC and Nehemiah in 445 BC. Ezra did a great deal to reform the worship that took place in the temple while Nehemiah saw to the rebuilding of the defensive walls of Jerusalem. They were encouraged in their work by another prophet, Malachi, with whom the Old Testament comes to a close.

The traditional view of the historical books after the Exile can be set out as follows:

§10. The Survivors

Although we still have the books of poetry and prophecy to fit into our jigsaw, the historical books of the Old Testament come to a close with Ezra and Nehemiah. But there are still 400 years

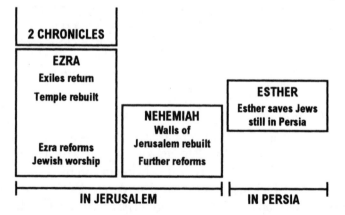

to go before we reach the New Testament and the time of Jesus. Another hole – more missing pieces in our jigsaw. Fortunately we can fill them in from other historical sources.

For over a century, Judea enjoyed a relatively peaceful and semi-independent existence as a province of the Persian

Empire. Then came Alexander the Great: heading east from Greece, he conquered all in his path, including the Persian Empire and, in 332 BC, the province of Judea.

Alexander died unexpectedly in 323, leaving his generals to fight for power. The Greek Empire was torn in half, divided between two great families, the Ptolemies (from Egypt to the south) and the Seleucids (from Syria to the north). Judea was the buffer zone in the middle and suffered for it. Between 323 BC and 198 BC the Ptolemies ruled Judea; the Seleucids ruled from 198 BC onwards, showing far less favour to the Jews than the Ptolemies had done.

One particular Seleucid king, Antiochus Epiphanes (Antiochus IV) invaded Judea and took Jerusalem. In 167 BC, believing himself to be divine, he desecrated the Temple by sacrificing pig's meat to Zeus on its altar – the 'abomination of desolation' prophesied in Daniel 9:27. This was too much for the Jews, who fought back. Led by members of the Maccabeus family, the Seleucids were unexpectedly defeated and the Temple reconsecrated.

It was under Greek rule that Jews living at any distance from Jerusalem started building synagogues as places for local worship. At the same time, different Jewish parties – such as the Pharisees and Sadducees – started to develop (see chapter 10 for details). Also significant was the translation of the Old Testament into Greek for the benefit of the Jews of the Dispersion – those living outside their Jewish homeland. This translation is called the Septuagint (abbreviated to LXX) and it is the version of the Old Testament most frequently quoted in the New.

Judea retained its semi-independence until another change of empire took place. In 63 BC, the Roman general Pompey took control of Judea, making it part of the Roman Empire. Under a grant from the Roman senate, Herod the Great (37-4 BC) was made King of Judea. It was under his rule that Jesus Christ was born.

§11. The Saviour – Jesus Christ

Jesus, God's Son, is the Bible's central character and its chief focus. The whole of the Old Testament is preparation for his coming. The four gospels tell us about his life, his teaching, his ministry, his death and resurrection. And the rest of the New Testament tells us about the salvation he came to bring. In such a limited space, it is impossible to do justice to his life, but I do recommend an end-to-end reading of an entire gospel at the earliest opportunity in chunk-reading fashion as described in chapter 3.

Except in a very broad way, the four gospels do not seek to give a chronological account of Jesus' life. Only two – Matthew and Luke – mention his birth. And only one records any event between his infancy and adulthood – Luke (2:41–52) tells of his visit to Jerusalem with his parents when he was twelve years old. All four concentrate on his public ministry, a period lasting just three-and-a-half years; and all four give their greatest attention to the events immediately before and after his cruci-fixion. Nevertheless, we can give an outline of Jesus' life:

His early life (recorded only in Matthew and Luke):
- Born in Bethlehem c. 6 BC (Matt 1:18–25, Luke 2:1–7)

- Visited by the shepherds (Luke 2:8–20) and, later, by wise men (Matt 2:1–12)

- Escaped from Herod to Egypt (Matt 2:13–18)

- Settled in Nazareth, aged perhaps four (Matt 2:19–23)

- Visited Jerusalem, aged twelve years (Luke 2:41–52)

His ministry:
- Baptised in the Jordan by John the Baptist c. AD 26 (Matt 3, Mark 1, Luke 3, John 1)

- Tempted in the desert (Matt 4, Mark 1, Luke 4)

- First miracle – water into wine at Cana in Galilee (John 2:1–11)

- Rejected at Nazareth, he made Capernaum his base (Luke 4:16–32)

- Began preaching in and around Galilee

- Called his disciples (Mark 3:13-19, Luke 6:13–16)

- Further preaching and miracles, mostly in Galilee

- Peter believes Jesus is God's Son (Matt 16:13–20, Mark 8:27–30, Luke 9:18–20)

- Jesus turns south, towards Jerusalem (Luke 17:11)

- Transfiguration (Matt 17:1–13, Mark 9:2–13, Luke 9:28–36)

His last week (AD 30 or 33):
- Triumphant entry into Jerusalem (Palm Sunday)

- Jesus turns the money-lenders out of the Temple

- Further teaching in the temple – the Jews again plot to kill him

- Last Supper and betrayal by Judas (Maundy Thursday)

- Garden of Gethsemane and arrest (Maundy Thursday)

- Trial, and denial by Peter (Thursday/Friday)

- Crucifixion (Good Friday)

His resurrection and beyond:
- Resurrection (Easter Sunday)

- Various resurrection appearances

- Ascension to heaven (forty days after resurrection)

- Pentecost: outpouring of the Spirit (fifty days after resurrection)

- His future return in glory – date unknown!

The gospels offer four pen portraits of Jesus and each is aimed at a slightly different audience. The first three, Matthew, Mark and Luke (sometimes called the Synoptics, meaning 'common view') overlap considerably and some gospel stories appear in two or all three accounts. John is more distinct. As you gain familiarity with the gospels, you will come to see the uniqueness of each, but this diagram gives a few pointers:

- **Matthew**, *the most Jewish of the Gospels, presents Jesus as a great teacher. There are many links with the Old Testament. Jesus emphasises that the Law cannot be broken and that he has come to fulfil it. Matthew frequently points out how Jesus, the coming King, is a fulfilment of OT prophecy.*

MATTHEW For Jews Jesus = teacher	Only Matthew & Luke record Jesus' birth	LUKE For Greeks Jesus = perfect man	
	MARK **For Romans** **Jesus = servant**	'orderly account' Jesus came 'to seek and save the lost'	**JOHN** **For Christians** **Jesus = Son of God**
Many OT quotes: **Jesus fulfils OT** **law & prophecy**	**John Mark got** **his information** **from Peter**	**Focus on the Spirit**	**theological account:** **'that you may believe'** **'I am' sayings;** **no parables**

- **Mark** *is the shortest of the Gospels and the pace is fast moving. Scholars think it was the first to be written. Many passages are seen from the point of view of Peter who probably asked Mark to write down Peter's eye-witness account of the life of Jesus. Mark emphasises that Jesus, God's obedient servant, is the Messiah, but the disciples are not to reveal this until after*

Jesus' victory over death.

- **Luke's Gospel** *is the most methodical and was written as 'an orderly account' (1:3). He shows how Jesus is central to God's plan of salvation for the whole world: Jew, Roman and Greek alike. He has a special interest in the action of the Holy Spirit and Jesus' work as the man of compassion among the poor. Luke wrote the Book of Acts as a sequel.*

- **John's Gospel** *emphasises the relationship between Jesus and the Father. Jesus is presented as eternal God. John sees Jesus' miracles as 'signs' that point to his true identity. There are no parables in John's Gospel, but he does include the 'I am ...' sayings of Jesus, e.g. 'I am ... the light of the world' (8:12); '... the Good Shepherd' (10:11); '... the true vine' (15:1).*

§12. The Christians

There remains one more historical book in the Bible: Acts – or to give it its proper title, The Acts of the Apostles. A better name might be the 'Acts of the Holy Spirit' because this book is all about what God the Holy Spirit was able to accomplish through the disciples after the resurrection. Acts was written by Luke, and is a sequel to the Gospel that bears his name.

Acts is the story of the early church, its successes and mistakes, its advances and the persecution it suffered. Only a few of the original twelve disciples are mentioned. Peter is the main character in the early chapters.

A significant verse is Acts 1:8. Jesus is speaking: 'You will receive power when the Holy Spirit comes on you; and you will be my witnesses in Jerusalem, and in all Judea and Samaria, and to the ends of the earth.'

Acts 2 records the outpouring of the Spirit on the disciples, giving them the courage to make Jesus known. Like concentric ripples spreading across a pool, Acts shows how the Gospel spread out from Jerusalem. Most significantly, the Church soon included Gentiles (non-Jews) as well as Jews, thus breaking across one of the most fiercely-held social and religious barriers of the time.

In chapter 9 we read of the conversion of Saul, a hard-nosed Pharisee bent on destroying the infant Church. Meeting Christ in a vision on the road to Damascus, he becomes Paul, a servant of Jesus and an apostle (meaning missionary or messenger) of the Gospel. After this, the rest of Acts is mostly taken up with Paul's travels and the growth of the Church.

Linked to the Book of Acts are the New Testament letters, many of which were sent to churches and individuals named in Acts. See chapter 8 for details.

It is, however, worth outlining the contents of Acts in more detail than the diagram above permits:

Contents of Acts

- Jerusalem: the coming of the Spirit (chapters 1,2)

- Jerusalem: the church grows (chapters 3–7)

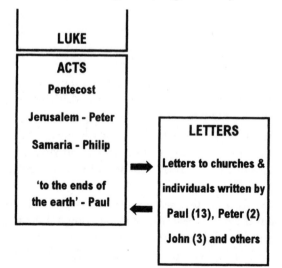

- Philip's mission in Samaria (8:1–25)

- The first African, an Ethiopian, converted (8:26–40)

- Saul converted, becoming the Apostle Paul (chapter 9)

- Cornelius, a God-fearing Gentile, converted (10:1 – 11:18)

- A Gentile church established in Antioch (11:19–30)

- Paul's escape from prison and death of Herod Agrippa (chapter 12)

- Paul's first mission, lasting two years (chapters 13,14)

- Church Council at Jerusalem, deciding the status of Gentile believers (chapter 15)

- Paul's second mission, lasting three years (15:30 – 18:22)

- Paul's third mission, lasting four years (18:23 – 21:17)

- Paul's arrest, trials and hazardous journey to Rome (21:18 – 28:31)

Many Bibles have maps showing the geographical spread of the Gospel outwards from Jerusalem and Paul's missionary journeys. Consult one if you can.

The Book of Acts closes with Paul under house arrest in Rome but still doing all he can to make Jesus known. Although not recorded in the Bible, Paul was put to death a few years later. But the story of the Church does not end there. It is still going on 2,000 years later. And it is a story that will not close until Jesus comes again to wind up human history and to take believing Christians to be with him in glory for ever.

[1] Red Sea: not where marked as the Red Sea on modern maps, but a place to the north of this, nearer the Nile Delta, and more accurately known as the Sea of Reeds. Its exact location is uncertain.

5

Deeper still: further approaches to Bible reading

THERE is more than one way to skin a cat – or so the saying goes. Personally, as a cat-lover, I cannot imagine why anyone would ever want to separate a feline from its outer covering! But there is certainly more than one way to read the Bible. In this chapter, we're going to look at three further approaches to Bible reading and study. Two more follow in chapter 6. Those in this chapter build on the basic Quiet Time approach set out in chapter 3. No one approach is better than another: indeed, a variety of approaches is the best route to a sound understanding of Scripture.

Crucial to every method of Bible reading and study is the correct interpretation and understanding of the text. Approach 4 will focus on this. Cynics assert that the Bible can be made to mean anything anyone wants it to mean. Regrettably, the Bible has been used to justify any number of atrocities that are embarrassing blots on the landscape of Christian history, but it is a complete fallacy to suggest the Bible can mean whatever a person wants it to mean. *A Bible passage can mean only one thing: what the original author, inspired by the Spirit of God, intended it to mean.* When the Bible is handled honestly, with humility and submissiveness to the Spirit of God, we won't go far wrong.

I once had to learn a hard lesson. As an enthusiastic but young and naive Christian I was eager to obey all God's commands. I came across these verses: 'You are all sons of light and sons of the day; we are not of the night or of darkness. So then let us not sleep, as others do, but let us keep awake and be sober' [1 Thess 5: 5–6, RSV].

I took this to mean Christians should not sleep but stay awake twenty-four hours a day! Three days and three entirely sleepless nights later, I collapsed into an exhausted heap. I concluded that my interpretation had been amiss. I had made several basic blunders. For one thing, I had taken the verses out of context: the passage is in fact about staying alert spiritually as the return of Christ draws closer. Nor had I weighed up my interpretation of these verses against other parts of the Bible. Psalm 127:2 would have made a useful comparison: 'In vain you ... stay up late ... for he grants sleep to those he loves.'

I had taken these verses too literally. And I had also failed to consult older and wiser Christians on their understanding of the passage. Had I done so, I might have saved myself some grief. Thankfully, no lasting harm was done, and I learnt an important lesson. But even today I cannot read 1 Thessalonians 5 without a wry smile to myself.

❧

Different approaches to Bible reading and study appeal to different temperaments. But taking a previously untried approach can open the Bible in a delightfully new and refreshing way. Whatever approaches are adopted, three things remain important. God's Word is spiritual food: we come to it to feed our souls, not stuff our minds. Second, both head and heart need to be receptive. Third, it must always be applied. We are to be *doers*, not merely *hearers* (see James 1:22).

Approach 4: In-depth study
In-depth Bible study builds on the Quiet Time reading approach we considered in chapter 3, but it goes further in seeking to get

to grips with Scripture's original meaning. An in-depth study is useful in itself, but is especially helpful as preparation for giving a talk or leading a group discussion. The danger of an in-depth study is to stop when we think we've understood the meaning of a passage: as with any other form of Bible reading, it must be applied. Tools to help with an in-depth study include comparing different Bible translations; using cross-references, a concordance, a study Bible and commentaries. These are described in more detail in chapter 9.

Here is a six-step approach I have found beneficial over many years:

1 Pray and read

2 Consider the context

3 Consider the construction

4 Interpret carefully, looking for the original meaning

5 Compare Scripture with Scripture

6 Look for God's message – and apply!

Our example is Psalm 23, given here with cross-references:

Psalm 23

A psalm of David.[a]

1 The LORD is my shepherd,[b] I
   shall not be in want.
  2 He makes me lie down in
   green pastures,[c]
he leads me beside quiet waters,[d]
  3 he restores my soul.
He guides me in paths of
   righteousness[e]
for his name's sake.
4 Even though I walk
   through the valley of the
   shadow of death,[f][n]
I will fear no evil,[g]
   for you are with me;[h]
your rod and your staff,
   they comfort me.[i]
5 You prepare a table before me
   in the presence of my
   enemies.
You anoint my head with oil;[j]
   my cup[k] overflows.
6 Surely goodness and love[l] will
   follow me
   all the days of my life,
and I will dwell in the house of
   the LORD forever.[m]

4 n Or *through the darkest valley*

a 1 Sam 17:12–15

b Isa 40:11; John 10:11,14;
   Heb 13:20; 1 Pet 2:25

c Ps 4:8; Ezek 34:14–15
d Isaiah 49:10

e Psalm 5:8, 78:72

f Psalm 138:7
g Psalm 27:1
h Ps 139:7-10; Is 43:2

i 2 Cor 1:3-4

j 1 Sam 16:13; Ps 92:10,
   104;15; Luke 7:46
k Psalm 16:5
l 2 Chron 6:41–42

m John 14:2

1. Pray and read

As with any reading or study of Scripture, we begin with prayer, signalling to God that we are open and submissive to his Spirit. Then we carefully read our designated passage.

2. Consider the context

No Bible verse or passage should ever be taken out of context. G. Campbell-Morgan, a wise and respected Bible teacher, once said, 'A text outside its context is a pretext.' We need to ask certain questions. Who wrote this? For whom? When? Why? What kind of writing is it? What is the setting of this passage? What comes before and after it? Answering these questions determines the *context* of a passage.

Psalm 23 was written by David, as indicated in the note at the top of the psalm. Significantly, David himself had been a shepherd before he became King of Israel. 1 Samuel 16:11,19 and 17:15 tells us this, and 1 Samuel 17:34–37 gives us more information about the kind of dangers David faced as a shepherd.

Like all the psalms, this is poetry. It is an expression of personal feelings, not a systematic setting out of doctrine. I'll say more about Hebrew poetry, with its parallel lines of thought, in chapter 7. Different kinds of writing – or genre – must be handled differently and interpreted appropriately.

As to when and why David wrote this psalm we can make an educated guess based on what we know of his life. Clearly, it is his testimony to the goodness and care of God. There were times when he was in fear of his life, such as when he was on the run from Saul or facing the Philistines in battle. He also carried the heavy responsibility of kingship. This psalm reflects his safe deliverance from difficult circumstances.

3. Consider the construction

Breaking a passage down into its component parts helps us follow its progression of thought and to see when new points are being introduced. This is especially important for passages where a line of argument is being carefully followed by the author. Paul's letters are a good example, where breaking a book into sections, and sections into paragraphs, is a beneficial exercise (see chapter 8 for an example). But even here, in Psalm 23, we can see two sections. The break comes between verses 4 and 5 where the picture changes from a shepherd with his sheep to a host with his guest. Many translations insert a blank line at this point to indicate the change in imagery.

4. Interpret carefully, looking for the original meaning

In an in-depth study we are particularly concerned to understand and interpret the text accurately. To do this we must get to its original meaning. Understanding what the author's words meant to their original audience is a necessary precursor to understanding what the Spirit is saying to us today. '*A text cannot mean what it never meant.*'[1]

It's important to check that we understand all the words and concepts used. In Psalm 23, there are phrases we need to grasp in order to see what the passage says. This comes before asking what it *means*.

For example, the 'valley of the shadow of death' in verse 4 may have overtones of a funeral service. But what is this valley? In Israel's deserts, there are some very steep-sided, rocky chasms. These afforded shade, water and grazing, but there was also an ever-present danger from wild animals and bandits lurking in the shadows. We can picture a shepherd guiding his sheep through such a place. The NIV has an alternative translation in the footnote: 'through the darkest valley'.

Then there is the rod and staff in verse 4: a rod was a shepherd's defensive club used to ward off wild animals; but a staff was a different kind of stick, used to control and guide the sheep. See how knowing this already adds to our understanding of the psalm: God both protects and guides. A commentary or study Bible will give this kind of background information.

Another question arises in verse 5. Oil poured on one's head?

An overflowing cup? Sounds messy! But in eastern cultures it was the custom for a host to provide olive oil to cleanse and moisturise the skin of those travelling under the hot sun. And an overflowing cup is a sign of generous provision.

In this psalm, these words and phrases relate to the cultural and historical background. In other parts of the Bible, it may be theological or technical terms we need to check out if we are to understand what the author is saying.

Having made sure we understand what the text says, we can move towards interpretation – understanding what it *means*. This involves grasping not just the author's words, but his thoughts. There is no foolproof set of rules of biblical interpretation. Common sense, familiarity with the Bible as a whole and experience count for a great deal, as does a careful and intelligent reading of what the text actually says. A good commentary can be a great help too. Here are some tips:

- The plain, most straightforward meaning of a text is generally the right one. Scripture contains revelation, not obfuscation! God's Spirit wants to open God's Word to us, not hide it from us.

- Having said that, the *plain* meaning of a passage is not necessarily its *literal* meaning. Psalm 23 is, after all, picture language set out in poetic form. Comparing God with a human shepherd does not exhaust our understanding of the character or work of God. God may be like a shepherd in some ways, but he is also much more than a shepherd.

- The original and plain meaning of a passage can often be illuminated by comparing one Bible version with another. Comparing a more literal rendering with a freer one can be especially helpful. Freer translations worth comparing include the Contemporary English Version, the New Living Translation and The Message (see chapter 9).

- Another 'trick' is to put the text into your own words. If you can express a Bible verse or passage in your own language with some confidence, it probably means you have grasped its original meaning.

As we seek to interpret and understand the text, there are certain clues to look for:

Look for the main ideas and points of emphasis
Try to determine the main idea(s) the writer is making, the central thrust of the message, and the line of argument that is being taken.

Look, too, for points that are emphasised. Often this is done through the repetition of words and phrases. In Psalm 23, the personal pronouns 'I' and 'me' and the personal adjective 'my' come some 17 times. This underlines the personal nature of the psalm and of the psalmist's relationship with God.

Look for contrasts and consequences
Looking for *contrasts, consequences, conditional promises, commands* and *invitations* is another good idea. You may not find all, or even any, of them; but if they are there, spotting them can add considerably to your understanding of a passage and its original meaning.

Bible writers make many contrasts: the way of the wicked contrasted with the way of the godly (eg in Ps 1); light contrasted with darkness (e.g. in 1 John); the fruit of the Spirit contrasted with sinful behaviour (eg in Gal 5:19–26).

Here, in Psalm 23, the contrast is between safety and danger. But it is not a simple contrast. God's protection comes not by his removing us from danger, but through his presence with us while we are in danger.

The Bible, both in its direct teaching and through the example of the lives it examines, spells out the likely consequences of the choices we make and the actions we take. Here, the result of putting our trust in God as shepherd is the certainty of his presence even in the most difficult circumstances.

Look for promises and their conditions:
As well as consequences of the kind, 'if this happens, then this follows,' we also find in God's Word many promises that are even more direct. God's promises, based on his covenant love, are usually conditional.

There are plenty of promises in Psalm 23: God's provision (v 1), his guidance and protection (vs 2–4), his overflowing blessing (v 5) and the security of his love (v 6). But in fact they are all *conditional* promises. They are conditional on the opening line: 'The Lord is my shepherd'. Only if I place my complete trust in God can I claim these promises for myself.

Look for commands and invitations
There are no obvious commands in Psalm 23, but there are plenty elsewhere throughout the Bible! We need to take God's commands very seriously indeed.

But what we do find is an invitation. In fact, the entire psalm is an invitation to put our whole-hearted trust in the Lord.

Look for examples, good and bad
The Bible presents us with many people portraits. There are bad examples to be avoided, good examples to be copied. In this psalm, David provides a positive role model of someone trusting God in difficult and dangerous circumstances.

Avoid allegory
Allegory divorces a passage from the writer's original intention in a dangerous way. An example might come from reading too much into verse 4: the reference to the shepherd's rod and staff. Because of the use to which these tools were put, they speak of God's protection and his guidance. However, I've heard the suggestion that the rod corresponds to God's law and that the staff corresponds to God's grace, drawing the conclusion that

God uses both in bringing us to salvation. While the conclusion in this instance is true (and can be demonstrated from elsewhere in the Bible), this is not what Psalm 23:4 is saying. It is going beyond our remit to force this interpretation on the psalm, attractive though it is. And very often conclusions drawn from an allegorical interpretation are wholly untrue!

Do be open to typology
Typology is different from allegory. Typology is when something – mostly in the Old Testament – is taken as a *type* or *pattern* anticipating an aspect of God's saving work in Christ. Typology, unlike allegory, does not divorce a passage from its original setting, but builds on it. Psalm 23 has an element of typology in that the work of a biblical shepherd is seen as prefiguring the compassionate pastoral work of Christ. Another good example of typology is in Genesis 22 – Abraham's near-sacrifice of his son Isaac. It clearly foreshadows God's provision of a substitutionary sacrifice – Christ, who died in our place to set us free from death.

5. Compare Scripture with Scripture
Making comparisons with other parts of scripture is a very important way of extending either a simpler quiet time reading or a more in-depth Bible study and also of ensuring we are interpreting our passage correctly. Three 'rules' apply:

- Always seek to interpret a difficult passage in the light of more straightforward passages. Don't work the other way around!

- Seek to interpret the Old Testament in the light of the New. There is a useful ditty to remember: 'Christ is in the Old concealed; Christ is in the New revealed.'

- Remember the Bible's teaching is self-consistent. Although one part of scripture may exhibit a more developed understanding than another (for example, the New

Testament has a much more developed understanding of life after death than is suggested by Psalm 23:6), scripture will never contradict itself.

Two alternative tools for comparing Psalm 23 with other parts of the Bible are a concordance (looking up 'shepherd' or other key words will locate other passages with a similar theme) and cross-references.

We are going to choose the latter option. Turn back to Psalm 23, printed above, and look at the cross-references found alongside.

The first, identified by a small raised *a*, leads to 1 Samuel 17:12–15. Looking this up, we find a passage which indicates King David was once a shepherd himself. The second, with the letter *b*, takes us to four further shepherd references. The most significant is John 10:11,14 in which Jesus declares himself to be the Good Shepherd who knows his sheep by name and is prepared to lay down his life for them.

As a further activity, why not look up some or all of the remaining cross-references for yourself?

6. Look for God's message to you

This is something to which we always have our eyes and ears open. After seeking to establish the original meaning of a passage, we must not neglect to consider what God may be saying to us. It might be a word of instruction, a challenge, a rebuke, a word of comfort, a message of encouragement or, as here, an invitation calling for a personal response of deeper trust. Psalm 23 has an easy-to-see personal application, but not all passages do. Look back to the end of chapter 3 for what was said there about outward, upward and inward means of application.

From Psalm 23 we can thank God for his care and protection. We can talk to him about our most deep-seated fears and the pressures we are under. We can find restoration and refreshment for our weariness. As we read the psalm again, we can find our faith lifted.

We could also use this passage as a vehicle of prayer for others, for those who are going through a tough time, who feel that life is closing in on them. Verse 4, with its reference to the valley of the shadow of death, would prompt me to pray for terminally ill members of church and family. May they know God's overflowing blessing as they face the enemies of disease and death; may they not fear the present or the future; may they know they are secure now and eternally, held in the arms of a loving shepherd.

Approach 5: Bible meditation

A quiet time reading engages head and heart. An in-depth study chiefly engages the head. Meditation focuses on the heart. The aim of meditation is to sink deep into God's words and to let God's Word sink deep into you. No specific tools are required other than a Bible, your imagination and perhaps a notebook to record your discoveries. However, even in Bible meditation we are not looking for fanciful interpretations of Scripture that bypass or overturn the rules of good interpretation. What we are doing is allowing the Spirit of God to speak more directly to us at a spiritual rather than a cerebral level.

Meditation is encouraged in Scripture. It builds up the believer (see Ps 1:1–3). We are invited to meditate upon:

- God's character:　　Psalm 48:9
- God's deeds:　　Psalm 77:12
- God's Word:　　Psalm 119:97

Psalm 23 will again be our starting point. Find a private place free from interruption. Begin with prayer. Submit yourself to the Holy Spirit. Become still and quiet before God (see Psalm 46:10). Hand any recurring or distracting thoughts over to him (see 1 Peter 5:7).

Read the psalm slowly, ideally out loud. Put yourself in the scene. See it in your mind's eye. You are emerging from a deep, dark valley. You can recall a frightening or stressful experience. But now you enter a grassy, sunlit meadow, a river running through. You splash your face with the cooling water. You drink deeply and quench your thirst.

As you rest on the grass by the riverbank, someone approaches. It is the Lord. He speaks to you. What does he say? He holds out a gift, a blessing. What is it? You decide. It can be whatever your heart most needs: an answer to a long-unanswered prayer; a gift of healing; a fresh outpouring of his Spirit; the restoring of your spiritual vigour. Take the gift from his hands. Receive it with thanks. Continue with this for as long as seems right. Then let the meditation come to a natural conclusion. End with thanksgiving.

❧

The parable of the two sons in Luke 15 that we considered in chapter 3 can work equally well as a meditation. Read the parable carefully. Then choose one of the characters, and in your mind's eye re-live the story from that perspective. Try to get inside the character's thoughts and feelings.

If you are the younger son, imagine how you feel at being lost; and at being welcomed home. If you feel far from God, allow this meditation to be the means of restoring your relationship with him. Or if you see yourself as the older son, consider how you feel about your brother's return and your father's invitation to join the party. The parable is unfinished – we don't know whether the older brother came in or stayed outside. You could supply your own ending as you respond to the invitation.

You could even be the waiting, watching father and in your mind's eye imagine a lost individual returning. Use this as a prayer for non-Christian friends and family members.

Ignatius Loyola, founder of the Jesuits, advised that all one's senses should be applied to meditation. We can see, hear, touch, even smell and taste the elements of our surroundings. Meditation is not a flight of fantasy. Because God's Word is living and because it reveals Jesus, it can be an actual encounter with the Lord. Any Bible story that can be visualised is suitable for this treatment. The parables of Jesus and the Gospel accounts of his healings are ideal.

Those who make meditation a regular part of their devotional lives may find it advisable to work with a spiritual friend or director in developing this kind of prayer, as it can touch a person's emotions quite deeply.

An alternative means of meditation for those unsure about using their imagination in the way I've suggested, is to ponder just one phrase of Scripture – though do look up the context first! John 14:27: 'My peace I give to you'; or John 15:4: 'Abide in me' – are eminently suitable.

Spend time turning the phrase over in your mind. To meditate means literally to chew the cud – like a cow! Let the words speak to you: not just to your mind, but also deep within your heart. Let Jesus' words bring healing to your spirit. Take the phrase with you into the day. Have it written up somewhere you can see it often so it can bring you back into the presence of God at any moment.

Meditation is not a substitute for other kinds of Bible reading, but it can complement them. In fact one can lead to another. After a detailed study of a passage, why not close the commentaries and study aids and let that same passage speak to you in an entirely different way?

Approach 6: Character study

When I worked as a journalist, I was constantly being told, 'Find the human interest in the story.' The Bible is full of human interest. Characters are very honestly portrayed. A character study focuses on just one individual and can be a very profitable means of study.

Sometimes a Bible character will be mentioned in just one

passage; sometimes his or her story will cover several consecutive chapters. Often, however, a character's story is scattered over several places. The first thing to do is to locate all the necessary information. A good concordance (or computer software with search facilities) will help do this. Our example is Nicodemus.

His story is found in John's Gospel. It comes in three places and builds up a progressive picture: John 3:1–21; 7:50–52 and 19:38–42. Look up and read these passages now. The most valuable is the first. Consideration of what Jesus has to say about being 'born again' would make a very worthwhile study in itself, but for now we are simply concerned with Nicodemus.

John 20:31 tells us the main purpose the author had in writing his Gospel: 'These [stories about Jesus] are written that you may believe that Jesus is the Christ, the Son of God, and that by believing you may have life in his name.'

In his Gospel, John tells us about people who make a journey of faith. He tells us how they find an interest in Christ and put their trust in him. We learn from John 3:1 that Nicodemus was a Pharisee and a member of the Sanhedrin, the Jewish ruling council. The Pharisees did not care for Jesus. He accused them of hypocrisy and showy religion and befriended the less religious types of which they disapproved. Nicodemus is an exception. He is genuinely curious about Jesus. He visits Jesus by night (3:2), perhaps fearful of being spotted by colleagues. Unlike other Pharisees who regarded Jesus as in league with the devil (see Matt 9:34; 12:24), Nicodemus acknowledged Jesus came from God and says he is impressed by the miracles Jesus had been doing.

But he doesn't understand the answers Jesus gives to his questions. What we have in John 3 is a record of the discussion but no indication of Nicodemus's response. We are left in suspense.

We next meet Nicodemus in John 7:50–52. The verses come at the end of a passage focusing on the identity of Jesus and the claims he's making. The Pharisees want him arrested (7:32), but the temple guards fail to carry out their orders (7:45–49). Nicodemus now makes a stand – reasonably diplomatic, but enough for his fellow Pharisees to question his loyalty to them. He asks for Jesus to be given a fair hearing. So something of what Jesus had said had sunk in! Nicodemus is now a step nearer faith, but still has to contend with the hostility towards Jesus from his fellow Pharisees.

The third and final mention of Nicodemus is in John 19:38–42, the account of the burial of Jesus' body after his crucifixion. It was Joseph of Arimathea, another Sanhedrin member (see Luke 23:50), who took the body of Jesus down from the cross, and Nicodemus helped him bury it. Normally, the corpses of crucified criminals were thrown into a common pit. If this had happened to Jesus, there would never have been an empty tomb to find on Easter Sunday.

Although Joseph and Nicodemus were only doing what decent Jewish custom demanded (v 40), their act was public and would have been carefully noted by other Pharisees and Sanhedrin members. Joseph provides the tomb; Nicodemus provides a generous amount of spices. Both are deeply sacrificial acts of devotion.

We are told Joseph was a disciple (v 38), albeit in secret. The description is not used of Nicodemus, and perhaps he wouldn't have acted as he did if Joseph hadn't taken the initiative. But Nicodemus's faith had definitely progressed. The fact he put his future career and public reputation on the line is clear evidence of this.

This is just one example of a simple character study. As before, application is all-important. Nicodemus's story tells us that finding faith is often a journey and a struggle, not something that necessarily happens in a single momentous event. In this respect, you might like to compare Nicodemus with Paul in Acts 9 whose conversion came in a flash of blinding light. And it has something to say to all Christians who find themselves in an environment that is hostile to the Lord Jesus and in which making a public stand might be costly.

Other suggestions for character studies can be drawn from the 'People' section of the excellent 'Rapid Finder' in the *New Lion Encyclopedia of the Bible*, edited by John Lane (see chapter 9, Tools of the trade).

[1] Gordon Fee and Douglas Stuart, *How to Read the Bible for all its Worth*, second edition, Scripture Union, 1994, p26.

6

The subtle approach: thematic methods of Bible study

THE approaches to Bible reading and study we considered in chapters 3 and 5 were largely *passage based*. In this chapter, we look at two more approaches that come at the Bible more subtly, tracing ideas and topics through the Bible as a whole. There are two kinds: the theme study which takes a biblical subject; and the contemporary study which addresses a modern issue of moral or ethical concern. Our two examples will be the authority of Jesus and the Christian use of Sunday respectively.

Approach 7: Theme study
A theme study takes a topic and follows this through different parts of the Bible, sometimes the whole Bible. The trick is to choose a theme that's neither too daunting nor too restricted. Our worked example will be of moderate size: the authority of Jesus. Naturally, our main hunting ground will be the Gospels.

The authority of Jesus
The hardest part of a thematic study is locating the right passages. A concordance is indispensable. An obvious starting point would be to find references in the four Gospels containing the word 'authority' or related words such as 'power'. This gives quite a few verses to work with. But a concordance will not pick up every occasion when Jesus acted with authority or power. Jesus clearly demonstrated his authority when he raised

Lazarus from the dead (John 11), but neither the word 'authority' nor the word 'power' are found in the passage. An especially valuable resource is *The NIV Thematic Study Bible*, published by Hodder & Stoughton, available in book form or as a CD-ROM. Using this, together with a concordance, I gathered the following information:

Jesus is seen as having authority:

- To teach. He taught as 'one having authority' and – pointedly – not like the teachers of the law (Mark 1:22).

- To forgive sin. 'Your sins are forgiven,' he said to the paralysed man lowered through the roof. The Jewish leaders and teachers thought this blasphemous: 'Who can forgive sins except God alone?' they said (Mark 2:1–12).

- To cast out demons. 'Even the evil spirits obey him,' people said (Mark 1:27). And when he did cast them out, the spirits acknowledged Jesus to be the Holy One, sent from God (Mark 1:24). The most notable of Jesus' exorcisms is the deliverance of Legion (Mark 5:1–20).

- Over the forces of nature. He turned water into wine (John 2:1–11); he fed crowds of 5,000 (Mark 6:35–44) and 4,000 (Mark 8:1–10); he walked on water (Mark 6:45–52); and he calmed a raging storm (Mark 4:35–41).

- Over disease. The Gospels record over thirty occasions when Jesus healed individuals and several more when he healed large numbers, in fact, 'all who came to him' (Matt 8:16).

- Over death. There are three occasions when Jesus raised the dead: Jairus's daughter (Matt 9:18,19,23–25); a widow's son (Luke 7:11–15) and his friend Lazarus (John 11:1–44). And he healed those on the point of death such as the centurion's servant (Matt 8:5–13; Luke 7:1–10). And, of course, he himself rose victorious from death on Easter Sunday.

A significant verse in which Jesus claims authority for himself is Matthew 28:18: 'Jesus came to [the disciples] and said, "All authority in heaven and on earth has been given to me."' Using a different tool, cross-references from this verse took me to several other passages both inside and outside the Gospels: 'All things have been committed to me by my Father' (Luke 10:22); 'The Father loves the Son and has placed everything in his hands' (John 3:35); 'Father, you granted [your Son] authority over all people that he might give eternal life to all those you have given him' (John 17:2).

These verses speak of the authority Christ exercised on earth. Yet others speak of the authority the ascended Christ has now (by virtue of his obedience to God in submitting himself to crucifixion) and which will be universally demonstrated on his return:

> [God] raised [Christ] from the dead and seated him at his right hand in the heavenly realms, far above all rule and authority, power and dominion, and every title that can be given, not only in the present age but also in the one to come. And God placed all things under his feet and appointed him to be head over everything (Eph 1:20–22).

> God exalted [Jesus] to the highest place and gave him the name that is above every name, that at the name of Jesus every knee should bow, in heaven and on earth and under the earth, and every tongue confess that Jesus Christ is Lord, to the glory of God the Father (Phil 2:9–11).

I even found an Old Testament passage in the cross-references:

> In my vision at night I looked, and there before me was one like a son of man, coming with the clouds of heaven. He approached the Ancient of Days and was led into his presence. He was given authority, glory and sovereign

power; all peoples, nations and people of every language worshipped him. His dominion is an everlasting dominion that will not pass away, and his kingdom is one that will never be destroyed (Dan 7:13,14).

The Ancient of Days is God, but in Daniel's vision a human being is brought before God and given eternal and universal authority. We take this to be Jesus. His favourite title for himself, 'Son of Man', appears in these verses, and the depiction of this person 'coming with the clouds of heaven' fits closely with Jesus' description of his own future return in glory (see Mark 13:26, 14:62). The theme could be extended further, but we have the basis for a valuable study into the person and work of Jesus Christ.

Studying a theme can open up all kinds of areas of interest. It's easy to be up all night checking and cross-checking references. It is wise not to extend a Theme Study too far, otherwise confusion will reign and application will be overlooked. Define your theme carefully and stick within its limits. Suitable subjects are legion. *The NIV Thematic Study Bible* offers over 2,000!

Approach 8: Contemporary study

A variation on the theme study is the contemporary study. Rather than taking a biblical topic, the starting point is a modern-day issue. Abortion, euthanasia, divorce, same-sex partnerships, concern for the environment and nuclear disarmament are just a few of the vexed moral and ethical issues facing Christians today.

The difficulty here is that the Bible may not give a direct or easily found answer. This is why Christians can and do arrive at different opinions on some issues. Sometimes Christians disagree because they're not prepared to accept the clear teaching of Scripture on an issue, but sometimes it's because Scripture doesn't tackle an issue in a direct way. The Bible does express a

view on homosexual relationships (a clear and consistent one in
my opinion), but it never mentions, say, nuclear disarmament.
It does, however, address issues of peace and justice, war and
self-defence, that give us principles to work from. It doesn't say
anything about abortion or euthanasia, but it does uphold the
sanctity of human life, made in the image of God. Other issues,
such as divorce and remarriage, are addressed in the Bible, but
the principles given don't by themselves cover every reason for
marriage breakdown we might meet today. We have to extrapo-
late from biblical principles to a working pastoral practice.

Space doesn't permit treatment of these examples here.
Suffice to say that while we want our thinking to be informed
by biblical precedent and principle, care must be taken when
beginning with what the Bible writers said to their own day and
applying it to our own time and culture. We will take one
worked example: the Christian's use of Sunday.

Working and shopping on Sundays

How we observe Sunday raises problems for Christians. Is it
ever right to work on a Sunday? Or to shop? In the church of
which I'm minister, some would feel uncomfortable about buy-
ing even a newspaper or a pint of milk on a Sunday; others
would not be unhappy spending the afternoon in a DIY store or
garden centre. There are Christians who work on a Sunday.
Some do shop work. Unnecessary perhaps? Others, such as doc-
tors, do vital life-saving work. Is there a difference?

Some things in the Bible are clear cut. Adultery, murder or
theft, for example, can never be justified. But if old friends drop
by at Sunday tea-time, is it wrong to nip out for a pint of milk
so we can offer them a cup of tea? Hospitality is a gift the Bible
encourages (Rom 12:13; 1 Pet 4:9). Or, if an elderly parent is in
hospital and you drive to visit them on a Sunday afternoon, is it
wrong to fill up with petrol in order to get there and back? The
fifth commandment, to honour one's father and mother, is as
important as the fourth, prohibiting as it does, work on the sab-

bath. As in the previous example, we must gather the biblical material, then ask how we apply it. I've used the same tools as before.

An obvious starting point is the Ten Commandments, the fourth of which says: 'Remember the Sabbath day by keeping it holy. Six days you shall labour and do all your work, but the seventh day is a Sabbath to the Lord your God. On it you shall not do any work' [Exod 20:8–10].

The injunction is principally against working. Nothing is said about either shopping or – for that matter – going to church (but see Lev 23:3 and Heb 10:25)! We could argue, however, that if we go shopping others are being made to work, and that this is wrong.

Turning to the New Testament, we find that Jesus' regular custom was to be in the synagogue on the sabbath (Luke 4:16). It is always a good principle to ask: What would Jesus do? And the early Christians set aside Sunday – the day Jesus rose from the dead – for worship (see Acts 20:7; 1 Cor.16:2; Rev 1:10). But the sabbath finds a much earlier reference in the Bible than either the Law of Moses or the practice of Jesus. Reflecting the Genesis account of creation (Gen 2:2,3), the fourth commandment continues: 'For in six days the Lord made the heavens and the earth, the sea, and all that is in them, but he rested on the seventh day. Therefore the Lord blessed the Sabbath day and made it holy' (Exod 20:11).

Establishing the sabbath as a day of rest was not just a law for God's people, but a creation principle for everyone. From this, many Christians argue that the churches should be striving to maintain Sunday as a special day for the whole of society, not just churchgoers. This principle lies behind the work of the campaigning group Keep Sunday Special.

But returning to what an individual Christian should do, we have found nothing yet that tells us precisely where to draw the line over what can and cannot be done on a Sunday. The prophets spoke about the sabbath too, and what they say is helpful for Christians in a secular environment. Amos, for example, criticised traders who couldn't wait for the sabbath to end so they could get back to making money (8:5). In a later historical book, Nehemiah told God's people not to buy any goods that foreigners came to sell on the sabbath (10:31; 13:15–22). Both Amos and Nehemiah have a pertinent message that we can relate to the issue of Sunday shopping.

In the Gospels we meet the Pharisees. They attempted to give an exact definition of what was and wasn't lawful on the sabbath. For example, travelling any distance greater than a sabbath day's journey – to the local synagogue and back – was outlawed. Jesus ran foul of these man-made regulations on several occasions. He and his disciples were once criticised for plucking ears of corn as they took a sabbath stroll. To show how petty the Pharisees' rules were, Jesus proceeded to heal a man with a shrivelled hand and then went on to make clear there was nothing wrong in doing good and saving life on the sabbath (Luke 6:8–11).

While the sabbath is important – Jesus upheld Old Testament law (Matt 5:18) – it is wrong to be over-legalistic and stand in judgement of others. But this may still leave us wondering where to draw the line for ourselves. One further Bible passage completes the picture. 'One person considers one day more sacred than another; another considers every day alike. Each one should be fully convinced in his own mind. He who regards one day as special, does so to the Lord' (Rom 14:5,6).

So the early Christians were divided on this issue too! For both Paul and Jesus, standing in judgement on others was at least as great a sin as infringing a strict sabbath. Paul, an ardent advocate of Christian liberty, leaves the matter up to individual conscience. But it is not a case of anything goes. We are to examine our priorities before the Lord and, having done so, we should live as consistently as possible.

There are wider implications that we have not considered: how the church might stand up for workers threatened with the sack if they refuse to work on Sundays; and how we set about protecting marriage and family life against the values of an increasingly materialistic society. But we can make the following summary of the Bible's teaching:

- God made all humans with an inbuilt need for regular rest from work. Christians will want to work for a society in which this is protected. And by their own example, they will want to show the importance of keeping one day special.

- Christians will want to make worship a priority in their lives.

- Christians should not judge one another or be over-legalistic.

- While Christians have individual liberty, they will want to remain distinctive in their witness and not be sucked in to the values of the world (see Rom 12:2).

- Every Christian should follow his or her conscience in this matter, while taking into account the sensibilities of other believers (see Rom 14:13).

In this exercise, I've shown how principles can be drawn from the Bible as a basis for making ethical decisions. It is rarely a case of quoting a verse or two as a proof-text: the teaching of Scripture as a whole needs to be weighed.

How we translate the teaching of the Bible into twenty-first century living isn't easy. The Bible is not, in that sense, a straightforward text book for Christian living. Christian maturity, the advice of other Christians, good Christian books[1], and individual conscience all come into play, though none should ever contradict Scripture.

[1] John Stott, *Issues Facing Christians Today* (revised edition, Marshall Pickering, 1999) shows how to integrate biblical principles with Christian thinking on a wide range of ethical and moral issues, including those listed at the start of this section.

7

Poets and prophets

There are some important books in the Bible still to be looked at – and we shall deal with the remaining books of the Old Testament – the poets and the prophets – in this chapter and those of the New Testament in chapter 8. You can if you want, use these two chapters for reference – information to dip into as and when you need it.

The Old Testament contains thirty-nine books. In the Big Picture we covered the first seventeen of these, the books of law and history. Here we deal with what's left: six books of poetry and sixteen of prophecy. I'll also say something about the nature of Hebrew poetry and a little on the interpretation of prophecy.

Books of Poetry and Wisdom (Job to Ecclesiastes, Lamentations)

These six books of poetry are very different from one another. Three of them, Job, Proverbs and Ecclesiastes fall into a special category of writing called 'wisdom literature'.

Job is a book about suffering and faith. It tackles the question, 'Why do bad things happen to good people?' We don't know when it was written, but Job himself probably lived around the time of Abraham. Job, whose family is killed and who is afflicted with suffering, argues strenuously with his so-called friends that his suffering is not a result of sin.

The storyline is found in the prologue (chapters 1,2) and epilogue (42:7–17). In between comes the poetry, taking the form of a series of debates. First, in three cycles of speeches, Job's words alternate with arguments made by his friends, Eliphaz, Bildad and Zophar. Next come a series of arguments put forward by Elihu (chapters 32–37). Finally, Job calls God to account and God responds by revealing his power in the wonders of creation (38:1 – 42:6). In the end, God blesses Job with more than he lost.

Psalms is a hymnbook and prayerbook rolled into one. The full range of human emotions is expressed in its songs and prayers: from the depths of despair to the sublimest heights of joy. David is the principal author of the 150 psalms.

Classifying the psalms

Some psalms fall into certain categories, but it's not possible to produce a watertight classification for every psalm. Like life, they are untidy! There are two basic moods in the psalms: there are psalms of praise and psalms of pleading. The writer is either happy or complaining – sometimes both at the same time!

Some psalms are very personal, expressing the cry of an individual in time of need; others are for national or community use. Some exalt God as Creator; others revere him as King. Some make confession for sin; others express thanksgiving. Some contain instruction; still others point to the coming Messiah.

Here are a few examples:

- Psalms to God as Creator: 8, 19, 90, 104

- Psalms looking to God as King: 9, 24, 48, 93

- Psalms of worship: 5, 29, 33, 94–100, 146–150

- Psalms of trust: 16, 23, 17, 91

- Psalms of anguish: 3, 42–43, 54–59, 139, 140

- Psalms of confession: 6, 32, 51, 102, 103, 130

- Psalms of victory: 18, 34, 44, 118

- Psalms of instruction: 1, 19, 119

- Psalms pointing to Jesus as Messiah: 2, 16, 22, 45, 72, 110, 118

A special group of psalms (120–134) are the 'songs of ascent' sung by pilgrims 'going up' to Jerusalem. The shortest psalm is 117. The longest is 119. The most popular is undoubtedly Psalm 23. Favourite psalms include: 8, 19, 46, 51, 95, 100, 103, 121, 139 and 145.

Proverbs extols the virtues of wisdom and wise living. After the opening chapters introduce the theme in a general way, a large number of pithy one-liners cover many subjects: pride, wealth and poverty, health, honest speech, family life, friendship, drink, sex and much more. There are several collections of proverbs from different sources within the book. Some of these collections are associated with Solomon (see 1:1, 10:1 and 25:1)

Ecclesiastes, a pessimistic book, is about the futility of life. There is a time, it says, for everything under heaven (chapter 3), but without God life is meaningless. Traditionally, the author of this book has been regarded as Solomon (see 1:1 and 1:12). 'Ecclesiastes' means 'the preacher'. Like Job and Proverbs, this book is categorised as wisdom literature.

The Song of Songs is an erotic love poem, extolling the wonders of sexual attraction and intimacy. There are at least two or three speakers and some editions of the Bible try to identify them, though this is largely conjecture. Some of it appears to be a bride dreaming of her forthcoming wedding. Like Ecclesiastes, the book is associated with Solomon. Some see in the book an allegory of God's love for his people or Christ's love for his bride, the Church. Also called the 'Song of Solomon' or 'Canticles'.

Lamentations is a series of five laments bewailing the collapse of Jerusalem in 586 BC, a funeral dirge for the city. Its poetry is an acrostic format, each line beginning with successive letters of the Hebrew alphabet. Lamentations is closely associated with the prophet Jeremiah which is why it is found with the prophecy rather than the other poets.

Poetry in motion

A great deal of the Old Testament is written in poetry. Not only are there the six poetic books listed above, but large parts of the prophetic books are in poetry too. Hebrew poetry doesn't use lines with rhyming words like traditional English poetry; instead, it has lines with rhyming ideas. This is called parallelism. There are three basic kinds, all with somewhat technical names:

(a) Synonymous parallelism. The second line echoes or reinforces the first:

Deliver me from my enemies, O God;
Protect me from those who rise up against me [Ps 59:1]

(b) Synthetic (or progressive) parallelism. The second line continues from the first:

The Lord looks down from heaven on humankind
to see if there are any who are wise, who seek after God. [Ps 14:2 NRSV]

(c) Antithetical (or opposing) parallelism. The second line contrasts with the first:

The memory of the righteous will be a blessing,
but the name of the wicked will rot. [Prov 10:7]

Occasionally, Hebrew poetry uses acrostic, each verse beginning with successive letters of the Hebrew alphabet. This is not easy to bring out in an English translation, but often a footnote draws attention to it. The longest acrostic poem is Psalm 119. The first eight verses all begin with *aleph* (A); the next eight with *beth* (B), and so on. Lamentations is another example of poetry in acrostic form. So too is Proverbs 31:10–31, a poem in praise of hard-working wives!

Books of Prophecy (Isaiah to Malachi)

There are a large number of prophets in the Old Testament. The life and teaching of some is found in the historical books. There is, for instance, Nathan who challenged King David on his adultery with Bathsheba (2 Sam 12); and Elijah who defied the false prophets of the god Baal (1 Kings 18). But there are others who have lent their names to the Old Testament books of prophecy. There are sixteen of these, from Isaiah to Malachi.

Four – Isaiah, Jeremiah, Ezekiel and Daniel – are known as the Major Prophets, not because they are more important, but because they are longer. (The small book of Lamentations, an appendix to Jeremiah, is dealt with above under the Prophets.) Unsurprisingly the remaining twelve are known as the Minor Prophets, on account of their generally shorter length.

Contrary to popular belief, the prophets did not spend all their time foretelling the future. Occasionally they do (some important passages that point towards Jesus are listed in chapter 10), but for the most part they address the people and the issues of their own day. The prophets constantly call the people and their leaders back to God. They warn of God's punishment, but equally make it clear that there is the certainty of forgiveness and restoration when God's people turn back to him.

Applying two questions fixes the position of each prophet in the Bible timeline:

- When did they preach?
- To whom did they preach?

There are three possible answers to each question

(a) As to when?

- Before the exile, ie in the time of the divided kingdom
- During the exile
- After the exile, ie in the time of the builders

(b) As to whom?

- To Israel (northern kingdom)
- To Judah (southern kingdom)
- To a foreign nation

The answers can be set out in a table:

	Israel	**Judah**	**Other**
Before the Exile (during the Kings)	Amos Hosea	Isaiah Micah	Jonah (to Assyria)
During the Exile		Zephaniah Habakkuk Jeremiah Ezekiel	Nahum (to Assyria) Daniel (to Babylon)
After the Exile (during the builders)		Haggai Zechariah	
Uncertain dates		Malachi Joel	Obadiah (Edom)

We can fit the prophets into the mid-section of our Bible time-line. Although Elijah and Elisha do not have Bible books named after them, I have added them because they are so important. Here is a brief introduction to each one, in approximate historical order.

Bible Timeline - Prophets

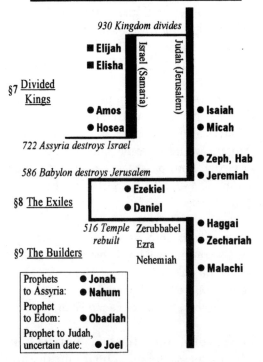

930 Kingdom divides

■ Elijah
■ Elisha

§7 <u>Divided Kings</u>

Israel (Samaria) | Judah (Jerusalem)

● Amos
● Hosea

● Isaiah
● Micah

722 Assyria destroys Israel

● Zeph, Hab

586 Babylon destroys Jerusalem

● Jeremiah

● Ezekiel
● Daniel

§8 <u>The Exiles</u>

516 Temple rebuilt — Zerubbabel
Ezra
Nehemiah

● Haggai
● Zechariah

● Malachi

§9 <u>The Builders</u>

Prophets to Assyria:	● Jonah ● Nahum
Prophet to Edom:	● Obadiah
Prophet to Judah, uncertain date:	● Joel

Amos and **Hosea** (c. 750 BC) both prophesied to the northern kingdom of Israel shortly before its destruction at the hands of the Assyrians. Both began prophesying in the reign of Jeroboam II; Hosea also preached to some of Jeroboam's successors. While Amos stressed the importance of social justice and respect for one's neighbour, Hosea called the people to love God. He showed them God's faithfulness and their own unfaithfulness by marrying Gomer, an adulterous wife whom he went on loving. 'Let justice roll on like a river, righteousness like a never-failing stream!' (Amos 5:24).

Isaiah began his work in 740 BC on the death of King Uzziah (6:1) which brought to an end a long period of stability.

Emphasising the sovereign power and holiness of God, he preached against corruption, but also promised future glory and victory over other nations. Chapters 9 and 11 contain important prophecies of a royal Saviour, taken by Christians to be Jesus. Chapters 36–39 (paralleled in 2 Kings 18–20 and 2 Chron 32) relate to the reign of King Hezekiah and the threat of the Assyrian king Sennacherib.

Chapters 40–66 have a different tone to the earlier part of the book. Some think they were written by another, later, prophet, but the two halves also have much in common. The prophecies in these chapters would have brought encouragement to the Jews living in exile. Four passages, known as the Servant Songs (42:1–4, 49:1–6, 50:4–9, 52:13 – 53:12) are taken as Messianic, ie referring to Christ.

> For to us a child is born, to us a son is given,
> and the government will be on his shoulders.
> And he will be called:
> Wonderful Counsellor, Mighty God,
> Everlasting Father, Prince of Peace (9:6).

Micah prophesied at much the same time as Isaiah. A much shorter book, his message highlighted injustice in the nation and corruption among its leaders.

> He has showed you, O people, what is good. And what does the Lord require of you? To act justly and to love mercy and to walk humbly with your God (6:8).

Joel was a prophet to Judah, but his date is unknown. He compared God's judgement with a devastating locust swarm, but goes on to promise a universal outpouring of God's Spirit, fulfilled on the day of Pentecost (see Acts 2).

> Afterwards, I will pour out my Spirit on all people.
> Your sons and daughters will prophesy,

> your old men will dream dreams,
> your young men will see visions.
> Even on my servants, both men and women,
> I will pour out my Spirit in those days (2:28,29).

Jonah and **Nahum** were both missionary prophets to Nineveh, capital of Assyria. Jonah is best known for his unconventional means of transport – a great fish! Both men said Nineveh would fall. The people of Nineveh listened to Jonah, repented and were saved, much to Jonah's annoyance. But later they refused to pay attention to Nahum. Assyria, as he prophesied, was swept away like a flood (612 BC).

> The Lord is good, a refuge in times of trouble.
> He cares for those who trust in him,
> but with an overwhelming flood
> he will make an end of Nineveh (Nahum 1:7,8).

Habakkuk complained, in the form of an argument with God, that the wicked were going unpunished. God's answer was that the Babylonians would punish Judah for her sins and that Babylon in her turn would be punished for excessive violence. 'The earth will be filled with the knowledge of the glory of the Lord, as the waters cover the sea' (2:14).

Zephaniah preached during the reign of King Josiah, and encouraged the spiritual reforms the king introduced. He told Judah that while the corrupt majority would be destroyed and exiled, an upright minority (a 'remnant') would be preserved.

> The land by the sea, where the Kerethites dwell,
> will be a place for shepherds and sheep pens.
> It will belong to the remnant of the house of Judah; there
> they will find pasture.
> In the evening they will lie down in the houses of Ashkelon.
> The Lord their God will care for them; he will restore their
> fortunes (2:6–7).

Jeremiah. The young Jeremiah, the 'weeping prophet', was called to preach in 626 BC during the reign of King Josiah, not long before the destruction of Jerusalem. Jeremiah warned his people not to court Egypt as an ally against the Babylonians and told them they would be taken into exile if they didn't turn back to God and put their trust in him. Few believed him and he suffered considerable hardship.

Jeremiah often used vivid pictures to make his point and even mimed some of his prophecies. For example, in the example of a potter remoulding a misshapen clay pot, he saw a picture of God destroying then remaking the nation (chapter 18). The prophecies and events recorded in Jeremiah – incidentally the longest book in the Bible – are unfortunately not in chronological or thematic order.

> The word of the Lord came to me, saying,
> 'Before I formed you in the womb I knew you,
>   before you were born I set you apart;
>   I appointed you as a prophet to the nations' (1:4,5).

Obadiah is the shortest book in the Old Testament. Its date is unknown, but Obadiah warns the nation of Edom (the descendants of Esau) of judgement, perhaps for not helping Judah fight off the Babylonians when they took the Jews into exile.

> You should not look down on your brother
> in the day of his misfortune,
> nor rejoice over the people of Judah
> in the day of their destruction (1:12).

Ezekiel lived among the Jewish exiles in Babylon. He gave strange visionary prophecies of hope that looked forward to renewal and God's blessing flowing from a rebuilt temple. One of the best known passages is his vision of a valley of dry bones that come alive (chapter 37). Ezekiel dated his prophecies very carefully. He was called in 593 BC and was active for at least twenty years.

> While I was among the exiles by the Kebar River, the
> heavens were opened and I saw visions of God (1:1).

Daniel also prophesied during the Exile, but his message was
to the Babylonians. He and his friends risked their lives to keep
the Jewish faith alive and uncompromised. The stories of the
fiery furnace (chapter 3) and the lions' den (chapter 6) come to
mind. Chapter 5 describes the judgement of King Belshazzar
and the destruction of Babylon. The second half of the book
contains visions about successive future empires.

> [Daniel's God] is the living God
> and he endures forever;
> his kingdom will not be destroyed,
> his dominion will never end.
> He rescues and he saves;
> he performs signs and wonders
> in the heavens and on the earth.
> He has rescued Daniel
> from the power of the lions (6:26,27).

Haggai and Zechariah both encouraged the returning exiles
(led by Zerubbabel and the high priest Joshua) to complete the
rebuilding of the Temple. Zechariah (9–14) also contains visions
looking forward to God's triumph and a future Messiah. "The
glory of this present house will be greater than the glory of the
former house," says the Lord Almighty' (Hag 2:9).

Malachi, meaning 'my messenger', warned the people against
empty worship and social corruption. He also deals with marriage to foreign wives (with its accompanying danger of idol
worship), a problem Ezra (chapters 9–10) and Nehemiah (chapter 13) faced at the same time. Finally, he foretells the coming
of another Elijah (John the Baptist in the New Testament), who
will prepare the way for the Messiah.

The Old Testament closes with Malachi. Between him and
John the Baptist lie 400 silent years during which there was no

prophetic revelation from God. "'Test me in this," says the LORD Almighty, "and see if I will not throw open the floodgates of heaven and pour out so much blessing that you will not have room enough for it'" (3:10).

Understanding and interpreting prophecy

In addition to what was said about biblical interpretation in chapter 5, there are special points to watch out for when reading the Bible's prophetic books:

- Understanding the original historical and political context of each book is vital. Before we can begin to apply what we find in the Bible's prophetic books to our own situation, we need to understand what the prophets were saying to the people of their own day. The notes given above indicate where each prophet fits into the overall framework of Old Testament history.

- The prophetic books are the record of what the prophets preached. 'Thus says the Lord,' is a recurring phrase. As preaching, prophecy contains many word pictures. It is dramatic and visual, and needs to be unlocked with the imagination. Getting the overall sweep of a prophetic passage is more important than grasping every last detail.

- The prophets emphasise God's sovereignty and the demands made by his holy character. The two 'moods' of the Old Testament prophets are judgement and hope: judgement for unfaithfulness to God and hope following repentance.

- The prophets judged Israel by the standards of the covenant. The two great covenant commandments can be summarised as Love God (Deut 6:5; Matt 22:37); and Love your neighbour (Lev 19:18; Matt 22:39). The prophets consistently condemn the breaking of these commands by idolatry and injustice.

- The prophets judged Israel's neighbours by their moral

failures and by how they treated God's covenant people.

- Very little prophecy is predictive. Douglas Stuart estimates that less than five per cent looks ahead to the New Testament; less than two per cent is messianic; and less than one per cent concerns events yet to come.[1] The majority of Old Testament prophecy comprised *forthtelling*, not *foretelling*. It primarily addresses concerns of the present, not the distant future. Although so little Old Testament prophecy is *predictive*, this did not prevent New Testament preachers and writers seeing it as *anticipatory*. Three examples are found early in Matthew's Gospel: 1:22,23 (Isaiah 7:14); 2:14–15 (Hosea 11:1); and 2:16–18 (Jer 31:15). Jesus is the fulfilment of Old Testament prophecy just as he is the fulfilment of Old Testament history, law and wisdom. (See Acts 13:32–37; 18:28; 24:14; 28:23; Rom 1:2,3 and 1 Cor 15:3,4.)

- Jesus himself believed that Old Testament prophecy bore witness to him. See, for example, Matt 5:17; 12:39–41; Luke 4:21; 24:27; 24:45 and John 5:39.

- In the days of the Old Testament prophets, God's people and the nation were one and the same. The nation, because of its covenant relationship with God, could be judged fairly by whether it had adhered to or strayed from the covenant stipulations. Today, church and nation are two separate entities. We need care in deciding what applies to the church and what applies to the world.

- Some Bible teachers suggest that Old Testament prophecy can have a double fulfilment, ie a further fulfilment in our own day in addition to an original fulfilment in Bible times. Claims to a double fulfilment usually focus on events in Israel and the Middle East. While it's true that New Testament writers saw a further fulfilment of Old Testament prophecy in Christ, it is generally unwise to look for timetables of future history based on Bible prophecy. Jesus specifically warned us not to speculate about dates or times (Acts 1:7). The one major unfulfilled biblical prophecy is the Second Coming of Christ.

[1] Fee and Stuart, *How to Read the Bible for all its Worth*, Scripture Union, p166.

8

Letters and more

FIRST, a word about the title of this chapter. 'Letters' is self-explanatory: we'll survey the twenty-one letters (or 'epistles') found in the New Testament. But what about 'more'? I refer to the final book of the Bible, one which leaves some Christians quaking at the knees – Revelation. All in good time, but first those letters.

New Testament letters

The New Testament contains twenty-one letters. Of these, the Apostle Paul wrote thirteen. Paul's letters all take their titles from the name of the church or individual to which they were sent. With one exception, the remaining letters are named according to their authors: one from James; two from Peter; no fewer than three from John; and one more from Jude. Because they were written to unspecified groups of Christians, the letters from James to Jude are called the General Epistles. The one remaining letter – Hebrews – is anonymous: it is barely a letter at all, more of a theological treatise.

Not all scholars agree on the authorship of all the letters. Some, for instance, question whether Paul penned Ephesians or if Peter wrote 2 Peter, but I'll stick to the traditional view that the letters are written by the authors to whom they are attributed in the New Testament itself.

Letters from Paul

We can put Paul's letters into three groups. We have nine letters written to churches, three to church leaders, and one personal letter.

Paul's letters to churches

With two exceptions (Romans and Colossians), Paul's letters were written to follow up a personal visit. Having evangelised a city or region, Paul later encouraged the infant churches under his care through his correspondence with them. Often the Book of Acts tells us how the church in question came into being. Where appropriate, the relevant references are given in brackets.

ROMANS (c. AD 57)

Romans is a letter full of Christian doctrine. It sets out Paul's position on God's plan of salvation for both Jew and Gentile. Having established that all are guilty before God and under his judgement, Paul explains that a sinner can only be made right with God ('justified') through God's undeserved love ('grace'). Abraham is an important example of this. No-one, Paul says, can be made right with God through good works or obedience to the law, but only through faith in God who offers new life as a free gift. The law simply shows how serious sin is and how guilty we are.

A highlight of Romans – indeed of the whole Bible – is chapter 8. The Christian is not under God's condemning wrath, but under grace. The Spirit gives new life, adoption as God's children, liberty from the law and victory in Christ.

Following this is a digression in chapters 9–11 on the subject of how Jew and Gentile each fit into God's saving plan. Chapters 12–15 call for consecrated living and transformed conduct. Finally, chapter 16 contains a long list of greetings.

• Paul wrote this letter before arriving in Rome as a prisoner.

    I am not ashamed of the gospel, because it is the power of

God for the salvation of everyone who believes: first for the Jew, then for the Gentile. For in the gospel a righteousness from God is revealed, a righteousness that is by faith from first to last, just as it is written: 'The righteous will live by faith' (1:16,17).

1 and 2 CORINTHIANS (c AD 54–57) [Acts 18:1–18]

The church at Corinth faced serious divisions and moral problems. There were questions about marriage, sexual morality, diet (in the context of eating meat offered to idols), worship, the Lord's Supper, spiritual gifts, Christian liberty and resurrection. These are all dealt with in 1 Corinthians. One of its most familiar passages is Paul's hymn of praise to love (chapter 13), but the letter begins with a discussion about wisdom:

> Jews demand miraculous signs and Greeks look for wisdom, but we preach Christ crucified: a stumbling block to Jews and foolishness to Gentiles, but to those whom God has called, both Jews and Greeks, Christ the power of God and the wisdom of God. For the foolishness of God is wiser than human wisdom, and the weakness of God is stronger than human strength (1 Cor 1:22–25).

The theme running through 2 Corinthians is the suffering and weakness of Paul himself. Apparently, some had questioned his effectiveness and authority as an apostle. Paul is happy to boast about his weaknesses through which, he says, God is able to display divine power. Paul describes his hardships with honesty yet says his concern for the churches is an even heavier burden (11:28). The letter includes an appeal for funds to help needy Christians in Jerusalem.

> [The Lord] said to me, 'My grace is sufficient for you, for my power is made perfect in weakness.' Therefore I will boast all the more gladly about my weaknesses, so that Christ's power may rest on me. That is why, for Christ's sake, I delight in weaknesses, in insults, in hardships, in

persecutions, in difficulties. For when I am weak, then I am strong (2 Cor 12:9–10).

GALATIANS (c. AD 48?) (Acts 13:14 – 14:24; 16:1–6; 18:23)
A group of 'judaisers' were telling the Galatian Christians they had to submit to the ritual laws of the Old Testament, including circumcision. Paul opposes this, arguing (as he does more fully in Romans), that believers are made right with God by faith, not good works. Appeal is made to the example of Abraham. The letter incorporates a vigorous defence of Christian liberty. A favourite passage is the fruit of the Spirit: 'The fruit of the Spirit is love, joy, peace, patience, kindness, goodness, faithfulness, gentleness and self-control' (5:22,23).

EPHESIANS (c AD 60) (Acts 18:19 – 20:1; compare Rev 2:1–7)
Like many of Paul's letters, this one is in two halves: teaching followed by practical application. Paul begins by describing the spiritual blessings we have in Christ and how new life in Christ is made ours by faith. The idea of God's choosing those he intends to save ('election') is strong in this letter, as is the theme of the church.

The practical section, beginning at 4:17, encourages church unity and godly living at home; and urges Christians to protect themselves with 'the whole armour of God':

> Be strong in the Lord and in his mighty power. Put on the full armour of God so that you can take your stand against the devil's schemes. For our struggle is not against flesh and blood, but against the rulers, against the authorities, against the powers of this dark world and against the spiritual forces of evil in the heavenly realms. Therefore put on the full armour of God, so that when the day of evil comes, you may be able to stand your ground, and after you have done everything, to stand (6:10–13).

PHILIPPIANS (c. AD 60) (Acts 16:12–40)

Joy is the key word in this letter, one of the warmest in the New Testament. Paul, in prison, says he cannot decide whether he wants to live or die. More than anything else, he wants the Gospel to advance. Chapter 2 contains a wonderful hymn praising Christ's humility and subsequent exaltation. In chapter 3, Paul encourages his readers not to trust religious status or to give in to the 'judaisers' (see Galatians), but to press on to know Christ and his resurrection power. Finally, he commands them to 'rejoice in the Lord always' (4:4):

> Rejoice in the Lord always. I will say it again: Rejoice! Let your gentleness be evident to all. The Lord is near. Do not be anxious about anything, but in everything, by prayer and petition, with thanksgiving, present your requests to God. And the peace of God, which transcends all understanding, will guard your hearts and your minds in Christ Jesus (4:4–7).

- See below for a fuller analysis of this letter.

COLOSSIANS (c. AD 60)

Colossae was evangelised not by Paul, but by Epaphras, a convert of Paul during the apostle's time at nearby Ephesus. Colossians, a sister letter to Ephesians, asserts that Christ alone is sufficient for complete salvation and that Christ reigns supreme above all other cosmic powers. Establishing this at the beginning of the letter, Paul goes on to warn his readers about a heresy which suggested they needed more than just Jesus for salvation. The second half deals with rules for Christian living, especially in marriage and raising children. 'Live a life worthy of the Lord and please him in every way: bearing fruit in every good work, growing in the knowledge of God' (1:10).

- The four letters of Ephesians, Philippians and Colossians, together with Philemon, are known collectively as the 'prison epistles': Paul was in prison when he wrote them.

1 and 2 THESSALONIANS (c. AD 51/52) (Acts 17:1–9)
The theme of Christ's second coming is prominent in both
these early letters. Clearly, the Thessalonians were expecting
Christ's return to be soon. In the first letter, Paul assures his
readers that believers who have already died will not be disad-
vantaged when Christ comes again. Meanwhile, those who
remain alive are not to be idle but responsible and active. The
second letter warns of disorder and lawlessness preceding
Christ's coming. Other themes in these two letters include
endurance under trial, sexual relationships, the church's worship and its community life.

> The Lord himself will come down from heaven, with a loud
> command, with the voice of the archangel and with the
> trumpet call of God, and the dead in Christ will rise first. After
> that, we who are still alive and are left will be caught up
> together with them in the clouds to meet the Lord in the air.
> And so we will be with the Lord forever (1 Thess 4:16–17).

Paul's letters to church leaders
This trio of letters are often called the 'pastoral epistles': they
were written to pastors and have much to say about church life
and leadership. All three were prompted by Paul's concern over
false teaching creeping into the churches.

1 and 2 TIMOTHY (c. AD 64; c. AD 66)
Timothy was a shy, young man, a convert and frequent travelling companion of Paul. Because false teachers were making
inroads into the church at Ephesus, Paul left Timothy there to
appoint trustworthy leaders and to reorganise church life in an
effort to protect it from heretical views. First Timothy includes
instructions on church life and worship, qualifications for
elders and deacons, advice for different groups in the church, a
warning against the love of money, and words of personal
encouragement to Timothy. Paul also stresses the importance
of scripture and preaching in maintaining the true faith.

Second Timothy again encourages the young leader, calling upon him to endure faithfully and not to fear the godlessness which will appear in the last days.

> Don't let anyone look down on you because you are young, but set an example for the believers in speech, in life, in love, in faith and in purity. Until I come, devote yourself to the public reading of Scripture, to preaching and to teaching (1 Tim 4:12–13).

TITUS (c. AD 62)

Titus was placed in charge of the church on the Mediterranean island of Crete. Nice work if you can get it! But, like Ephesus, the church on Crete faced danger from false teaching. The letter looks at the duty of church leaders and church members, and the conduct of Christians as good citizens. There is considerable overlap with 1 Timothy. Titus 3:4–7 is sometimes called the Gospel in miniature:

> When the kindness and love of God our Saviour appeared, he saved us, not because of righteous things we had done, but because of his mercy. He saved us through the washing of rebirth and renewal by the Holy Spirit, whom he poured out on us generously through Jesus Christ our Saviour, so that, having been justified by his grace, we might become heirs having the hope of eternal life.

Paul's one personal letter
PHILEMON (c. AD 60)

Paul wrote this short and touching letter to Philemon, a church leader at Colossae, asking him to go easy on Onesimus, a runaway slave Paul was returning. Evidently, the slave had become a Christian while in Paul's company and had proved very useful to Paul who was in prison. Paul drops a mighty big hint he would like to keep the slave permanently. 'Welcome him as you would welcome me' (1:17).

Letters from other writers

HEBREWS

Although some older Bibles mistakenly attribute this letter to Paul, the identity of the author remains a mystery. The letter is addressed to Jewish converts. As such, it provides an important bridge between the Old and New Testaments. The Old Testament is liberally quoted.

The author shows how our new covenant in Jesus fulfils and supersedes the old. Jesus is portrayed as God's obedient and suffering Son who now reigns with God. A major theme is that of Christ as High Priest 'after the order of Melchizedek' (a priest-king who lived in the time of Abraham and before the written Law of Moses was given). As well as being our great High Priest, Christ is also the sacrifice for sin, an unrepeatable once-for-all-time offering. Because he is sinless, but still able to sympathise with sinners, Jesus is the perfect sacrifice. A favourite section is Hebrews 11, a chapter cataloguing Old Testament heroes of faith: 'Faith is being sure of what we hope for and certain of what we do not see. This is what the ancients were commended for' (11:1,2).

JAMES

James is a practical, down-to-earth letter. It echoes the Old Testament book of Proverbs. It wasn't written by James the disciple – he was martyred early on (see Acts 12:1,2) – but by another James, quite probably James the brother of Jesus and a key leader in the Jerusalem church.

James tells us that faith without works is dead and that God's Word must be obeyed as well as heard. He reminds us of the difficulty and importance of bridling the tongue. In the final chapter, he directs his attention to healing, faith and prayer. 'Do not merely listen to the word, and so deceive yourselves. Do what it says' (1:22).

1 and 2 PETER

These two letters are very different from each other. First Peter was written to young Christians facing persecution. Peter tells them they are a chosen people and must follow the example of Christ in suffering for doing good. It shows evidence that Peter knew the writings of Paul such as his letter to the Ephesians.

The subject of 2 Peter is Christ's Second Coming. Some false teachers were scoffing at this belief because Jesus had not returned soon enough. The writer says God's slowness is because of his mercy: God wants to give everyone a chance to respond to the Gospel.

> Praise be to the God and Father of our Lord Jesus Christ! In his great mercy he has given us new birth into a living hope through the resurrection of Jesus Christ from the dead (1 Pet 1:3).

> Do not forget this one thing, dear friends: With the Lord a day is like a thousand years, and a thousand years are like a day. The Lord is not slow in keeping his promise, as some understand slowness. He is patient with you, not wanting anyone to perish, but everyone to come to repentance (2 Pet 3:8–9).

- Partly because the early verses of 2 Peter 2 correspond so closely to the letter of Jude (see below), some scholars doubt if Peter wrote this letter. But it does claim to have been written by him (1:1) and the author says he was an eyewitness to Jesus' transfiguration (1:16–18). Perhaps Peter quoted Jude, or vice-versa.

1, 2 and 3 JOHN

These three letters have much in common with the Gospel of John, suggesting all four were penned by the same person. The letters were written against a background of false teaching which claimed Jesus only *appeared* to be human. John, by now

an old man and perhaps the last person alive to have known
Jesus personally, writes to correct this mistaken view.

Love for God and love for one another are major themes in
1 John. Second and Third John are much shorter. Second John
warns against the Antichrist, and says false teachers should be
turned away from the church. Third John praises Gaius in his
stand for the truth, while warning against the power-hungry
Diotrephes.

> Whoever does not love does not know God, because God
> is love. This is how God showed his love among us: He
> sent his one and only Son into the world that we might live
> through him. This is love: not that we loved God, but that
> he loved us and sent his Son as an atoning sacrifice for our
> sins (1 John 4:8–10).

JUDE

This brief letter from Jude, the brother of James and, by impli-
cation, of Jesus as well, is an attack on false teachers and an
encouragement to Christians to persevere to the end. Verses
4–16 closely parallel 2 Peter 2:1–8. 'Dear friends, although I was
very eager to write to you about the salvation we share, I felt I
had to write and urge you to contend for the faith that was once
for all entrusted to the saints' (Jude 3).

Interpreting the New Testament letters

> [Paul's] letters contain some things that are hard to
> understand (2 Pet 3:16).

Having looked briefly at each letter, there are some points
worth remembering when it comes to understanding and
applying the letters of the New Testament:

• The letters we have represent only one side of a two-sided
  correspondence between author and recipients. For example,
  in 1 Corinthians it is clear that Paul is answering questions

raised by the Christians at Corinth. But we can only make an educated guess as to exactly what their questions were and what were the precise circumstances that led to them being raised with Paul. Mostly, the letters were written to encourage Christians under fire or to correct some error in doctrine or practice. The concern of the writers is primarily pastoral, not abstract theology.

- Always read the whole of a letter before studying any one part of it in detail. Having a working outline is extremely useful. When reading any part of the Bible, attention to its construction is important. This is especially true of New Testament letters.[1] If possible, work with a book outline, either your own or a commentator's. Breaking a letter down into sections and sections into paragraphs helps to unravel the author's train of thought. An example of analysing a letter's construction is given below:

Analysing a letter: Philippians

A study Bible (see chapter 9 for recommendations) will give an introduction to each book of the Bible. This will do three things:

1 discuss matters of authorship, date and the circumstances under which the book was written

2 give an overview of its major themes

3 give an outline of its contents.

A commentary will do the same, but in more detail.

This type of information is especially helpful when it comes to the letters of the New Testament where understanding the circumstances and construction of the letter are particularly important to reliable interpretation.

Valuable though someone else's efforts are, there is no substitute for doing the groundwork ourselves. And it should be borne in mind that a commentator's assessment of issues such as authorship and date will be strongly shaped by their theological outlook.

Suppose, as an example, we want to study Paul's letter to the Philippians. The first thing to do is to read it right through – in chunk-reading fashion as described in chapter 3. Then we can begin to sort out answers to some basic questions such as: who wrote it? To whom? Why? When? In what circumstances? For what purpose?

1 Who wrote it? According to 1:1, it was Paul (with greetings from Timothy).

2 To whom did he write it? According to the same verse, to the Christians at Philippi. The letter is directed to the whole church, but it is the church leaders who are to take particular note of its contents. Philippi was a Roman colony and the Philippian Christians were nearly all Gentiles, which explains why there are no Old Testament quotations in this letter.

3 What do we know of the background? We know, from Acts 16:11–40, that Paul planted this church. He and Silas were imprisoned there. The first convert in Philippi was Lydia, a businesswoman from Thyatira who traded in expensive purple cloth.

4 Paul wrote this letter from prison (1:13,17). Paul didn't know whether he would be released or executed (1:19–21). He was writing to thank the Philippians for their financial support (1:5; 4:10–19). He commends Timothy and Epaphroditus whom he was sending to them (2:19,25). It was Epaphroditus who had brought the Philippians' gift to Paul (4:18).

5 Major ideas? Paul wants to encourage the Philippians in the face of persecution (1:29,30). He urges them to remain humble (2:1–5) and united (1:27; 4:2–3) in order to withstand this opposition. He warns them against false teachers (chapter 3)

and against those who preach the gospel with mixed motives (1:15–18). The command to 'stand firm' comes twice (1:27; 4:1).

6 Overall impressions? Philippians is one of the most joyful and warm letters Paul wrote. Unusually, he has no complaints to make about this church. Thanksgiving and joy (see 4:4) are its hallmarks.

Many of Paul's letters follow a common form of construction: introduction; a prayer of thanksgiving; doctrinal matters; practical application; and closing greetings mentioning various individuals. Most importantly, practical application arises out of a doctrinal basis. 'You believe this ... therefore live like this' is how Paul generally proceeds. Practical sections begin, for example, at Romans 12:1; Galatians 5:1; Ephesians 4:17 and Colossians 3:1. This pattern is not quite so easy to see in Philippians, but it is there. We can now make an outline of Philippians:

1:1–2	Paul's greetings
1:3–11	Paul's thanksgiving and prayer for the Philippians:
1:3–8	Thanksgiving
1:9–11	Prayer
1:12–26	Paul's life-threatening circumstances
1:27–2:18	The Philippians' circumstances
	Paul urges conduct worthy of the Gospel:
1:27–30	Stand firm and united in the face of opposition, but
2:1–5	remain gentle and humble towards one another,
2:5–11	following the example of Christ:
2:6–8	his stooping in humility
2:9–11	his lifting to glory
2:12–18	Further instructions on behaviour that bears witness to the Gospel
2:19–30	Recommendation of Paul's fellow-workers:
2:19–24	Timothy
2:25–30	Epaphroditus
3:1– 4:9	The Philippians' circumstances again
	The foolishness of trusting in religious status:

3:1–4a	Circumcision and other rituals give no advantage
3:4b–14	as Paul's own example shows
3:15 – 4:1	Maturity means standing firm as citizens of heaven
4:2–3	Paul's plea to two quarrelling church members
4:4–9	Paul's call to rejoicing, prayer and holy thinking
4:10–20	Paul's thanksgiving for the Philippians' gift and support
4:21–23	Paul's closing words and blessing.

The Bible was not originally written in chapters and paragraphs as ours are today. The chapter divisions especially are not always a good guide to the construction of a Bible book. Neither should you rely too much on the cross-headings found in newer Bibles. There is never just one way of making a book outline. But having one, preferably your own, helps considerably in understanding the author's purpose and in following his line of thinking.

Something more: Revelation

The last book of the Bible is one many Christians avoid for as long as possible. Its language seems bizarre. There is nothing else like it in the New Testament: it has more in common with the visionary sections in Old Testament prophets like Daniel, Ezekiel and Zechariah, all major sources for the symbolism found in Revelation. Of the 404 verses in Revelation, 278 contain one or more allusions to Old Testament passages, a massive seventy per cent! Revelation is a blend of letter, prophecy and a style of writing known as apocalyptic.

An alternative title for Revelation is *The Apocalypse*, a word meaning 'unveiling'. Imagine a curtain being drawn aside to reveal what is behind and you get the idea. And that is what Revelation is, a behind-the-scenes glimpse of what is taking place in heaven in parallel to earthly events (compare Eph 6:12).

Apocalyptic is different from straightforward prophecy in three important respects:

- Prophecy deals with God's action within history; apocalyptic looks forward to the end of history.

- Prophecy is spoken; apocalyptic is written (see Rev 1:19). Apocalyptic is a special form of literature, and how the contents are arranged is almost as important as the contents themselves. It was usually anonymous or attributed to a hero of the past. In this respect, Revelation is an exception, its author being identified as the Apostle John.

- Apocalyptic is deliberately cryptic. It is presented in the form of visions and dreams; its imagery is drawn from the realm of fantasy, not reality.

Revelation was probably written towards the end of the reign of the Roman Emperor Domitian (AD 81–96), the first to systematically persecute the church. 'Babylon' is a coded reference to Rome.

The number 'seven' – the number of perfection – is important. We have seven lampstands, seven stars, seven letters to seven churches, seven seals, seven trumpets, seven angels, seven thunders, a seven-headed monster, seven last plagues, seven bowlfuls of God's wrath, and so on. Some scholars think we can divide the book into seven sections; others see fewer than this. The divisions are not obvious.

Various schemes for interpreting Revelation have been put forward. Most are unnecessarily complicated. While the book begins with letters to contemporary churches and ends with a vision of Christ's return, no attempt should be made to fit the book into some kind of calendar of history. The Book of Revelation is made up of a kaleidoscopic series of overlapping scenes. These should be taken as running in parallel, not consecutively

Each scene describes the spiritual or heavenly battle between the forces of light and darkness in which the church is caught up. As the book progresses to its climax – the establishing of

God's universal rule – successive scenes become more vivid, and the reader is drawn further in. But it is the overall impression of the scenes, rather than the detail, that we should concentrate upon. Enjoy!

> I saw a new heaven and a new earth, for the first heaven and the first earth had passed away, and there was no longer any sea. I saw the Holy City, the new Jerusalem, coming down out of heaven from God, prepared as a bride beautifully dressed for her husband. And I heard a loud voice from the throne saying, 'Now the dwelling of God is among people, and he will live with them. They will be his people, and God himself will be with them and be their God. He will wipe every tear from their eyes. There will be no more death or mourning or crying or pain, for the old order of things has passed away' (21:1–4).

[1] Several books that suggest approaches to the interpretation of different biblical genre are given at the end of chapter 9.

9

Tools of the trade

Do your best to present yourself to God as ... a worker
who correctly handles the word of truth (2 Tim 2:15).

A modern translation of the Bible

THE one essential tool for Christian growth we've been discussing in this book is the Bible itself. Other 'tools of the trade'
have their uses, but the Bible is basic. Choosing a Bible, however, is not such an easy task. There are over twenty English
translations on the market, and each comes in a wide range of
editions. In choosing a Bible the first decision to make is 'which
translation?'

Many people, when they think of 'the Bible', mean the
Authorized Version which dates from 1611. It is also known as the
King James Version after King James 1 of England (James VI of
Scotland) who commissioned it. But although it is a wonderful
part of the heritage of English literature, the Authorized Version
cannot be recommended for everyday use. Many of its words and
phrasings are no longer understandable and in the nearly four
centuries since it was published modern scholarship has revealed
a better understanding of the underlying Hebrew and Greek man-
uscripts. It is far better to use a Bible in modern English.

Some churches have a particular version they use in their
worship and for other meetings. Using the same translation as
the church you attend would be a good choice. Other than that,

it is largely a matter of personal preference. The following modern versions can all be recommended:

- **New International Version**
  The most widely used modern translation first published in the UK in 1979. Very popular. 'Accuracy, beauty, clarity and dignity' are its stated aims. Many study tools use the NIV as their basis. A balanced translation: neither over-literal, nor too free. Since 1997 some UK editions have adopted gender-inclusive language.

- **New Revised Standard Version**
  Published in 1990, a revision of a revision of a revision (!) of the Authorized Version. Highly thought of for its accuracy. A good Bible for close study. More literal than the NIV. A scholarly word-for-word translation that is 'as literal as possible, as free as necessary'. Its immediate predecessor was the Revised Standard Version (1952). Oxford University Press publish NRSV editions with British spelling.

- **Good News Bible**
  Ground-breaking when it appeared in 1976, the GNB was the first major translation to move away from 'Bible English' in favour of more everyday language. Very much a thought-for-thought rendering rather than a word-for-word translation. Editions from 1994 onwards have gender-inclusive language.

- **Contemporary English Version**
  The CEV (published in 1997) builds in the principles of the GNB and has won the coveted Crystal Mark Award from the Plain English Campaign. Very readable and easy to understand. Free from theological words. God's 'grace' becomes God's 'kindness'.

- **New Living Translation**
  A thoroughgoing revision published in 1996 of the once-popular **Living Bible**. Clear and readable, and since 2000

available with British spelling. More vivid in style than most other translations. A further revision is in progress.

Here is Ephesians 2:8–10 in these five translations:

NIV (inclusive): For it is by grace you have been saved, through faith – and this not from yourselves, it is the gift of God – not by works, so that no one can boast. For we are God's handiwork ['workmanship' in non-inclusive editions], created in Christ Jesus to do good works, which God prepared in advance for us to do.

NRSV: For by grace you have been saved through faith, and this is not your own doing; it is the gift of God – not the result of works, so that no one may boast. For we are what he has made us, created in Christ Jesus for good works, which God prepared beforehand to be our way of life.

GNB: For it is by God's grace that you have been saved through faith. It is not the result of your own efforts, but God's gift, so that no one can boast about it. God has made us what we are, and in our union with Christ Jesus he has created us for a life of good deeds, which he has already prepared for us to do.

CEV: You were saved by faith in God, who treats us much better than we deserve. This is God's gift to you, and not anything you have done on your own. It isn't something you have earned, so there is nothing you can boast about. God planned for us to do good things and to live as he has always wanted us to live. That's why he sent Christ to make us what we are.

NLT: God saved you by his special favour when you believed. And you can't take credit for this. Salvation is not a reward for the good things we have done, so none of us can boast about it. For we are God's masterpiece. He has created us anew in Christ Jesus, so that we can do the good things he planned for us long ago.

Some translations are more literal, word-for-word translations. Others are freer and, in contrast, are known as thought-for-thought (or dynamic equivalence) translations. A third approach is the paraphrase – a version that is very free indeed. Usually the work of one person rather than a committee, paraphrases attempt to render the biblical text as expressively as possible. Often there will be a strong element of personal interpretation.

Two older paraphrases are JB Phillips's *New Testament in Modern English*, published in 1958, revised in 1972. Another is Kenneth Taylor's *Living Bible* (1971), of which the *New Living Translation* is a revision in the form of a translation rather than a paraphrase. A more recent example is Eugene Peterson's *The Message*. The New Testament and much of the Old Testament from Job onwards is already available: the complete Bible is due in 2001–2. Of the three, JB Phillips is arguably the best.

As a rule of thumb, word-for-word translations are more suited to detailed study; thought-for-thought versions are easier to understand and better for general and 'chunk reading'; and paraphrases can be fun to dip into occasionally when

BIBLE VERSIONS

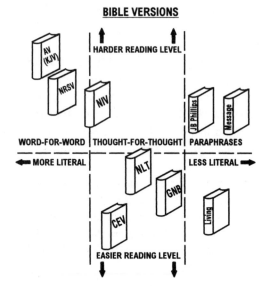

looking for a fresh insight into a familiar passage. The graph (p 140) makes some comparisons according to ease of reading (vertical scale) and degree of freedom (horizontal scale).

Browse through a number of versions before deciding which to buy. Better still, borrow one and use it for a week or two. Take advice from friends and church leaders. A Christian bookshop, with its specialist knowledge and larger range, is a better place to buy a Bible than a general bookshop.

To begin with, one Bible translation is sufficient, but after a while many Christians find it helpful to have a second so they can compare the same passage in two or more different translations. If you start with a word-for-word translation, consider complementing this with a thought-for-thought translation, or vice-versa.

Books of the Apocrypha

Some editions of the Bible contain extra books. These are known collectively as the Apocrypha or the 'deuterocanonical' books, meaning books of secondary authority. They were written in Greek, mostly in the period between the Old and New Testaments.

For those interested, the *Cambridge Annotated Study Apocrypha*, edited by Howard Kee (and published by Cambridge University Press), gives the full text of these books together with useful background information. A brief summary is also given on page 240 of the *New Lion Encyclopedia of the Bible*.

Concordance

A concordance is an alphabetical index of words found in a Bible, together with a Bible reference and a brief indication of the context. After a good translation, a concordance is the single most useful reference tool to have. It helps the Bible student do two things: to locate half-remembered verses and to conduct word and theme studies.

Concordances are specific to each Bible translation. Some Bibles and study Bibles have a concise concordance built in, but sooner or later, the serious Bible student will want something more comprehensive. The advantage of a more exhaustive concordance published as a separate volume is that it lists every occurrence of every important word in the Bible. Some even indicate the original Hebrew or Greek word underlying the English translation.

However, a better investment might be one of the commercially available pieces of Bible computer software. Usually on a CD-ROM, these provide the means for on-screen searches, including complex searches not easy to perform with a printed concordance. For example, I know there is a verse that tells me 'the Lord is good'. Looking up either 'Lord' or 'good' in a printed concordance would have me searching for hours. Using a computer search to find the phrase 'the Lord is good' turned up just eight verses and I quickly found the one I had in mind: 'Taste and see that the Lord is good' (Psalm 34:8).

Cross-references

Cross-references, placed alongside the text of the Bible itself, take the student from one part of the Bible to other places where a similar idea, word or phrase is to be found. We followed an example of cross-references to Psalm 23 in chapter 5.

Cross-references appear either in the margin, at the foot of the page or in a centre column. One would never want to look up every cross-reference to a given passage, but a consideration of the more significant can greatly enrich one's study. A cross-reference Bible is a thoroughly worthwhile investment.

Wide-margin Bibles

Some special Bibles have extra wide margins so you can add notes alongside the text. Good for the well-organised person. Other people like to underline or highlight verses that speak to them, but it is easy to forget why you underlined a particular bit and some people I know end up underlining almost every verse in their Bibles! If you are a margin scribbler or fond of underlining, consider keeping a Bible just for this.

Red-letter Bibles
Some Bibles (usually American editions) print the words of Christ in red. If you like it, fine. Personally, I think they are best avoided! The whole Bible is God's word.

Study Bibles
Special editions of the Bible offer study information. They usually have cross-references and may also include a short concordance. But the study notes, the main reason why such Bibles are bought, will offer some or all of the following:

- Introductions and outlines to each book of the Bible.

- Background information on geography and historical, cultural or religious practices.

- An explanation of theological words and ideas.

- A brief commentary, explaining the meaning of the text.

- Alternative interpretations of difficult passages.

- Charts, maps and timelines. Dates for biblical events.

- Personality profiles.

- Ideas for personal application.

There are a number of excellent study Bibles on the market. Choose one you think will meet both your present and future needs, one that is not too weighty but not so lightweight that you will soon grow out of it. And remember:

- Every study Bible has a theological viewpoint. The ones listed here are evangelical: they uphold traditional Christian doctrines and accept the historical reliability of the

Scriptures. Other study Bibles might cast doubt on the historical nature of some Bible miracles or the authorship of certain Bible books.

- The notes – even evangelical ones – are not infallible. You can disagree with the editor's opinion!

Among study Bibles that can be recommended are the following:

- *The Good News Study Bible*
  Excellent, and based on the easy-to-understand GNB translation. Simple, straightforward notes with some cross-references. Published by HarperCollins.

- *The Life Application Bible*
  Available in several translations including the NIV and NLT. Published by Tyndale. Emphasis is on application as well as information. Good use of sketch maps and thumbnail character profiles. The NLT edition is also available on CD-ROM.

- *The New International Version Study Bible*
  Highly respected, very thorough study notes, good concordance, plentiful cross-references. Conservative evangelical stance. Published by Hodder & Stoughton. Available on CD-ROM as part of The NIV Study Bible Library software package.

- *The NIV Thematic Study Bible*
  A different kind of study Bible. No interpretative notes, but marginal references linked to a 600-page thematic section, allow the user to trace any one of 2000 themes through the pages of the Bible, thus comparing scripture with scripture. Published by Hodder & Stoughton; also available on CD-ROM.

Of the above, I would recommend the first two for those new to the Bible and the last two for those not so new or very keen to learn more. A chart compares the features:

Study Bibles	Study notes	Book intros	Cross-refs	Theme refs	Concordance	Charts/maps	Timelines	People profiles	Application
Good News Study Bible	✓	✓	✓			✓			
Life Application Bible	✓	✓	✓		✓	✓	✓	✓	✓
NIV Study Bible	✓	✓	✓		✓	✓	✓	✓	
NIV Thematic		✓		✓		✓			

Reading Notes

We have already seen the usefulness of daily reading notes and how to make the best use of them in chapter 3. There are four principal publishers of reading notes in the UK.

- Scripture Union
  207/209 Queensway, Bletchley, Milton Keynes MK2 2EB
  website: www.scriptureunion.org.uk

- Bible Reading Fellowship
  St Peter's Way, Sandy Lane West, Oxford OX4 4HG
  website: www.brf.org.uk

- Crusade for World Revival
  CWR, Waverley Abbey House, Waverley Lane, Farnham, Surrey GU9 8EP
  website: www.cwr.org.uk

- International Bible Reading Association
  1020 Bristol Road, Selly Oak, Birmingham B29 6LB
  website: www.ncec.org.uk

A website covering all Scripture Union and Bible Reading Fellowship materials as well as books from other Christian publishers can be found at www.christianbookshop.com

Any Christian bookshop should be able to show you a range of Bible reading notes; alternatively ask your church leader for more information.

Commentaries

Commentaries do what their name suggests: they make comments on the Bible. A commentary examines the background and meaning of the text in a more detailed way than is possible in a study Bible. There is an almost overwhelming choice. There are one-volume commentaries covering the entire Bible and there are more detailed commentaries that tackle just one Bible book. Some are heavyweight scholarly tomes; others are written at a more introductory level. As with study Bibles, every commentary is written from a particular theological standpoint.

It is hard to make recommendations, but three series that offer application as well as interpretation are:

- The *Bible Speaks Today* series, published by IVP. Those by John Stott have been turned into study guides suitable for group use.

- *The People's Bible Commentary* series, from the Bible Reading Fellowship. These can be used as daily reading notes.

- The *Crossway Bible Guides*, published by Crossway Books (IVP). These are suited to group as well as personal use.

Among one-volume Bible commentaries, the following can be recommended:

- *The New Lion Handbook to the Bible*, published by Lion.

- *The New Bible Commentary (21st Century edition)*, published by IVP.

Bible reference books

There is a whole host of dictionaries, encyclopedias, handbooks and introductions offering a wealth of information for the Bible student. Those recommended here are for the beginner and/or intermediate student and are of an evangelical outlook.

Some offer articles in alphabetical order with entries on the books of the Bible, major Bible characters, places, history, customs and major themes. Others have much the same material but arrange it differently, either in chronological or biblical order.

Recommendations (from simplest to hardest):

- John Bowker, *The Complete Bible Handbook*, by Dorling Kindersley.

- John Drane (ed.), *The New Lion Encyclopedia of the Bible*, Lion.

  Both of these are extremely well laid out. Either would be an excellent investment, but you might not want both as there is a fair degree of overlap.

- John Drane, *Introduction to the Old Testament*, Lion.

- John Drane, *Introduction to the New Testament*, Lion.

- *The Illustrated Bible Dictionary* (three volumes), published by IVP/Tyndale. More heavyweight still. Articles are in alphabetical order.

- *The New Bible Dictionary*, published by IVP.
  Same as the Illustrated Bible Dictionary, but without the pretty pictures!

For younger readers (and adults wanting an easier life), there are:
- Eric Gower (ed.), *Look into the Bible: a Young Person's Guide*, Scripture Union.

- Robert and Ro Willoughby, *Children's Guide to the Bible*, Scripture Union.

Bible Atlases

A relevant map can be a great help in understanding the geography behind a particular Bible story. A map can give the route of the exodus, the layout of Jerusalem or the journeys of Paul as well as the location of places in the Holy Land and Near East.

Separate Bible atlases are available, but for most purposes the maps found at the back of Bibles that have them are entirely sufficient. Most study Bibles have maps.

Computer software and Internet sites

There is a wide range of Bible study software available. Typically, these provide one or more Bible translations linked to commentaries and other reference works. Four benefits of such software, over and against printed reference works are:

- The ability to have on-screen information alongside the biblical text.

- The ability to jump rapidly between one reference tool and another.

- The ability to perform sophisticated Bible searches (as mentioned above under 'concordances').

- The relative cheapness of electronic reference material and its compact size.

This is a fast-changing market and it is not easy to make firm recommendations. The CD-ROM version of *The NIV Thematic Study Bible* has already been mentioned, as has *The NIV Study Bible Library*, containing the contents of the printed *NIV Study Bible*, a very thorough commentary and much more besides.

Some program-writers like to cram their CD-ROMs with as many reference works as possible. This is not necessarily a good idea: the plethora of material can be too much. Be especially wary of programmes that have a large number of older reference and devotional works.

Two companies that offer catalogues of Bible software are:

- Sunrise Software, PO Box 19, Kingstown Broadway, Carlisle CA3 0HP. Website: www.sunrise-software.com
- Exousia Ltd, 53 Hindes Road, Harrow HA1 1SQ
  Website: dspace.dial.pipex.com/town/square/am28/index.html

There are literally thousands of websites providing an almost overwhelming amount of study material. Even new Bible translations are being developed specially for the web. The same advice and caveats apply as for bought software. One good starting point is the Goshen site at www.biblestudytools.net

Walk Thru' the Bible
Not something to buy, but an event to attend. Walk Thru' the Bible Seminars are an exciting way to get to grips with the big picture of the Bible. Using a series of handsigns and other memory aids, the seminar leader takes a group through the timeline of either the Old or New Testament. Look out for one in your area, or find the nearest from Walk Thru's website. Contact

- Walk Thru' the Bible Ministries, Thorpe-le-Soken, Essex CO16 0AA. Website: www.charis.co.uk/bible

Bibliography
In addition to the resources already listed, the following books can be recommended. First, those that help with understanding and interpreting the different types of writing found in the Bible:

- Stephen Motyer, *The Bible with Pleasure*, second edition, IVP/Crossway, 1997

- Gordon Fee and Douglas Stuart, *How to Read the Bible for all its Worth*, second edition, Scripture Union, 1994

- Richard Briggs, *Be an Expert in Interpreting the Bible*, Scripture Union, 1998

Of these three, Motyer's book is at an intermediate level, while Fee and Stuart's is more advanced. Briggs' *Be an Expert* is humorous and lively while still dealing with important ideas. Other titles that explore difficult genre and ways of reading Scripture include:

- Philip Yancey, *The Bible Jesus Read*, Zondervan, 1999

- David Wenham, *The Parables of Jesus*, IVP, 1989

Other books on the Bible:

- Andrew Reid, *Postcard from Palestine*, second edition, Good Book Company, 1997

- John Stott, *Understanding the Bible*, Scripture Union, 1972, revised 1984

- John Stott, *Evangelical Truth*, IVP, 1999 especially chapter 1: The Revelation of God

- Michael Riddell, *God's Home Page*, Bible Reading Fellowship, 1998

Books on developing your Quiet Time:

- Allan Harkness, *Ready to Grow*, Scripture Union, 1989, revised 1999

- Stephen Eyre, *Time with God,* IVP, 1995

Further books on prayer:

- Richard Foster, *Prayer,* Hodder & Stoughton, 1992

- Joyce Huggett, *Listening to God,* Hodder, 1986, revised 1996

- O Hallesby, *Prayer,* Hodder, 1936 and many reprints since

- Bill Hybels, *Too Busy Not to Pray*, IVP, 1998 (expanded edition)

10

Trainspotter's guide

THIS chapter is for people who like lists, facts and figures. Trainspotter or not, these quick reference items will prove useful to most Bible students sooner or later.

Abraham's family tree

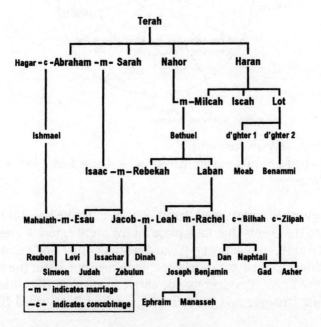

The tribes of Israel mostly take their names from the sons of Jacob (renamed Israel). They are Reuben, Simeon, Levi, Judah, Dan, Naphtali, Gad, Asher, Issachar, Zebulun and Benjamin. Joseph did not give his name to a tribe, but his two sons – Ephraim and Manasseh – each counted as half a tribe. The tribe of Levi provided priests for the Tent of Meeting and later for the Temple; they did not possess any land in Canaan.

Jewish calendar

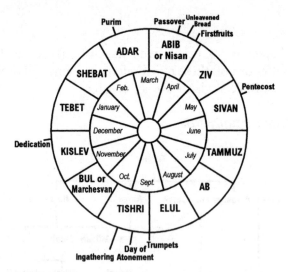

Annual Jewish festivals

Israel had a number of annual festivals. Those found in the Law of Moses are:

Passover and Unleavened Bread. Passover (Abib/Nisan 14) celebrated the events that took place on the night before Moses led the Isrealites out of Egypt. It was a reminder that God's destroying angel had 'passed over' Israelite homes but killed the firstborn of Egypt. Passover was celebrated with a sacrificial lamb. During Passover and the following week of Unleavened Bread

(Abib/Nisan 15–21), only bread made without yeast was eaten, a reminder that the Israelites didn't have time to wait for their dough to rise when they left Egypt. Jesus was crucified at Passover, thus the Christian Easter coincides with Passover.

Hebrew name: *Pesach*

References: Exod 12; Lev 23:5; Num 9:1–14; Deut 16:1–8; 2 Chr 30,35; Ezra 6:19–22; 1 Cor 5:6–8.

Firstfruits (Abib/Nisan 21). Held on the last day of Unleavened Bread. The first sheaf of the barley harvest was presented to God.

References: Lev 23:9–14, see 1 Cor 15:20–23.

Weeks (Pentecost, Harvest). The Festival of Weeks (Sivan 6) was the main harvest festival, celebrating the gathering of the wheat crop. It came to be known as Pentecost because it took place fifty days after Passover. It was the third of the three annual festivals that all Jewish males were obliged to attend, the other two being Passover and Ingathering. Christians remember the coming of the Holy Spirit at Pentecost.

Hebrew name: *Shavuoth*

References: Exod 34:22; Lev 23:15–21; Num 28:26–31; Deut 16:9–12.

Trumpets. Coming at the start of the seventh month, Trumpets (Tishri 1) announced the end of the agricultural year and prepared the way for the celebration of the Day of Atonement. Trumpets (or shophar), made of rams' horns, were blown to announce a day of complete rest.

After the exile, Trumpets became a New Year festival.

Hebrew name in modern times: *Rosh Hashanah*

References: Lev 23:23–25; Num 29:1–6; Neh 8:2–6.

Day of Atonement (Tishri 10). The most solemn day in the Jewish year. Israel confessed the sins of the past year and asked for God's cleansing. It was the only day in the year when the High Priest could enter the Holy of Holies, the innermost room of the Tent of Meeting, later of the temple. The sins of the people were symbolically transferred to a 'scapegoat' which was sent into the wilderness, a sign of the complete removal of the people's sins.

Hebrew name: *Yom Kippur*

References: Lev 16; Num 29:7–11; Heb 13:11,12.

Ingathering (Tabernacles, Shelters or Booths). A popular and joyful festival. It was held after the autumn fruit had been gathered in. For a week (Tishri 15–21), people lived outside in huts made from the branches of trees, a reminder of the time when the Israelites lived in the desert. Jesus' transfiguration took place during this festival, hence the disciples' desire to make shelters for Jesus, Moses and Elijah.

Hebrew name: *Succoth*

References: Exod 23:16b; 34:22b; Lev 23:33–36, 39–43; Num 29:12–39; Deut 16:13–15; Ezra 3:4; Zech 14:16–19; John 7:2.

Two further festivals were added later in biblical history:

Purim (Adar 14–15). A celebration of Esther's courage which led to the deliverance of the Jews threatened with extinction in the fifth century under Persian rule.

Reference: Esther 9:18–32.

Dedication (or Lights). A commemoration (on Kislev 25) of the re-dedication of the Temple by Judas Maccabeus in 164 BC after it had been desecrated by Antiochus Epiphanes. See chapter 4 'Big Picture' §10. Also called Lights because of the lamps placed in synagogues and homes.

Hebrew name: *Hanukkah*

Reference: John 10:22.

Places of worship

Initially, the people of Israel worshipped at places where they had special encounters with God. Often a heap of stones or an altar was the only visible sign.

A year after they escaped from Egypt (the exodus), they constructed the Tent of Meeting or tabernacle. This was their place of worship during their years of wilderness wanderings and under the rule of the judges.

After that there were three temples, all in Jerusalem:

- Solomon's temple. Dedicated for use in c. 960 BC; destroyed by the Babylonians in 586 BC.

- The second temple, built by the Jews returning from exile under the leadership of Zerubbabel and Joshua. Completed in 516 BC; desecrated by the Greeks in 167 BC; and destroyed by the Romans in 63 BC.

- The third temple, built by King Herod the Great. Begun in 19 BC, the main structure was ready by 9 BC, but finishing touches were still being added in AD 64. Destroyed, as Jesus predicted, by the Romans in AD 70.

Judges of Israel

The judges of Israel, as found in the Book of Judges, are listed below. These all followed Joshua and came before Samuel and the kings of Israel. It is likely that some of the judges, being local leaders, overlapped with each other. An exact chronology cannot be reconstructed.

Name of judge	Tribe or place of origin	Principal enemy	Years of oppre-ssion	Years of peace	Reference (in Judges)
Othniel	Judah	Aram	8	40	3:7–11
Ehud	Benjamin	Moab	18	80	3:12–30
Shamgar		Philistines			3:31
Deborah (and Barak)		Canaanites	20	40	chs 4,5
Gideon	Manasseh	Midianites	7	40	chs 6–8
Tola				23	10:1,2
Jair	Gilead			22	10:3–5
Jephthah	Gilead	Ammonites	18	6	10:6 – 12:7
Ibzan	Bethlehem			7	12:8–10
Elon	Zebulun			10	12:11,12
Abdon	Ephraim			8	12:13–15
Samson	Dan	Philistines	40	20	chs 13–16

Kings of Judah and Israel

Three kings reigned over the united kingdom before its division in 930 BC:

	Saul	1050–1010 BC
✓	David	1010–970 BC
	Solomon	970–930 BC

After the division of the kingdom in 930, Judah (to the south) and Israel (to the north) each had its own monarch. All dates are BC:

Judah (Jerusalem):		Israel (Samaria):	
Rehoboam	930–913	Jeroboam I*	930–910
Abijah	913–910		
✓ Asa	910–869	Nadab	910–909
		Baasha*	909–886
		Elah	886–885
		Zimri*	885
		Tibni*	885–880+
		Omri*	885–874+
✓ Jehoshaphat	869–848	Ahab	874–853
		Ahaziah	853–852
Jehoram	848–841	Joram	852–841
Ahaziah	841		
Athaliah (queen)	841–835	Jehu*	841–814
✓ Joash	835–796	Jehoahaz	814–798
✓ Amaziah	796–767	Jehoash	798–782
✓ Azariah (=Uzziah)	767–740	Jeroboam II	782–753
		Zechariah	753–752
		Shallum*	752
		Menahem*	752–742
		Pekahiah	742–740
✓ Jotham	740–732	Pekah*	740–732
Ahaz	732–716	Hoshea*	732–722
✓ Hezekiah	716–686		
Manasseh	686–642	+Tibni and Omri were
Amon	642–640	rivals for the throne until
✓ Josiah	640–609	Omri gained the upper
Jehoahaz	609	hand in 880 BC
Jehoiakim	609–597		
Jehoiachin	597		
Zedekiah	597–586		

A ✓ indicates those kings of Judah who are praised in the Bible. A * by the name of a king of Israel indicates he took the throne by force, not by right of succession. Because of overlapping reigns and the way some kings reckoned their period in office, the reign of some kings may appear shorter than stated in the Books of Kings and Chronicles.

Jewish religious and political parties

Between the Old and New Testaments, while Judea was under Greek and then Roman rule, various religious and political groupings were formed. All wanted to preserve the Jewish faith and nation, but some (notably the Pharisees, scribes and zealots) sought to achieve their aim by opposing the ruling powers while others (notably the Sadducees and tax collectors) did so by seeking compromises with their overlords.

Scribes were originally employed to copy the Scriptures and legal documents, and they became the professional interpreters in matters of OT law and teaching. In the OT, Ezra was a godly scribe. In NT times most scribes belonged to the party of the Pharisees. Some sat on the Sanhedrin (see below). Also called 'lawyers' or 'teachers of the law'.

Pharisees meticulously followed OT law and their own additional regulations. They were influential in the synagogues. Ultra-conservative, very strict, nationalistic and separatist, they stood against compromise. Jesus often accused them of hypocrisy, but one Pharisee, Nicodemus (John 3) asked Jesus how he could find eternal life. The Apostle Paul was a converted Pharisee. The name Pharisee means 'separate'.

Sadducees were political compromisers. Drawn mostly from the aristocracy, they were supporters of Herod. They only accepted the first five books of the OT (the Law of Moses) and did not believe in resurrection, an after-life, angels, demons or a future Messiah (see Matthew 22:23 and Acts 23:8). They were dominant in Temple life and the Sanhedrin. The chief priests were nearly all Sadducees. Sadducee means 'righteous'.

Sanhedrin was the ruling Jewish Council and supreme law court. Made up of seventy men and presided over by the High Priest. Jesus was tried before the Sanhedrin, but only the Roman governor Pilate could pass the death penalty.

Essenes are not directly mentioned in the Bible. The Essenes lived a simple communal life. Monklike, they followed strict rules of conduct and were mostly unmarried. The majority lived in desert settlements. They didn't take part in the temple worship but had their own purification rites. They observed the sabbath strictly and venerated Moses. The famous Dead Sea Scrolls, found at Qumran, were written by a group very like the Essenes. Some think John the Baptist may have been influenced by the Essenes or was even one of them.

Zealots – a radical group, committed to the violent overthrow of the Romans and to bringing in an earthly Jewish kingdom. Jesus had a disciple called Simon the Zealot.

Tax collectors were Jews who collected taxes on behalf of the Romans. They were often extortionate as they were allowed to keep any profit they made. Regarded as collaborators by other Jews. Called 'publicans' in the Authorized Version of the Bible. Matthew (also called Levi) was a tax collector who became a disciple of Jesus (Matt 9:9). Another, Zacchaeus, had his life radically changed when he met the Lord (Luke 19:1–10).

Herod and his family tree

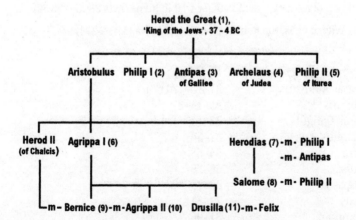

Notes:
(1) Herod the Great, 'King of the Jews' (37 – 4 BC), ruled all Palestine at the time of Jesus' birth (Luke 1:5). He ordered the killing of every infant male in Bethlehem (Matt 2:1–20). On his death, his kingdom was divided into four 'tetrarchies' and shared between three of his sons.

(2) First husband of Herodias (Mark 6:17).

(3) Tetrarch of both Galilee and Perea (4 BC – AD 39). Imprisoned and beheaded John the Baptist. Jesus called him 'that fox' and was sent before him by Pilate (Luke 3:1,19; 9:7–9; 23:7–12).

(4) Tetrarch of Idumea, Judea and Samaria (4 BC – AD 6). His presence in Judea was why Joseph took the infant Jesus to Galilee (Matt 2:22).

(5) Tetrarch of Iturea and Trachonitis (4 BC – AD 34). Married Salome (Luke 3:1).

(6) Grandson of Herod the Great, he ruled most of Palestine as 'King of Judea' (AD 37–44). He had James the Apostle put to death and imprisoned Peter (Acts 12:1–24).

(7) Granddaughter of Herod the Great. She married first Philip I, then Antipas (Philip's half-brother). John the Baptist was put to death for condemning this second marriage (Matthew 14; Mark 6; Luke 3:19).

(8) Daughter of Herodias. She danced before Antipas (Matt 14:6,7; Mark 6:21,22).

(9) Wife of Herod of Chalcis, then had an incestuous relationship with her own brother, Agrippa II (Acts 25:13).

(10) Son of Agrippa I. Sent Paul for trial in Rome (Acts 25:13 – 26:32).

(11) Wife of Felix, the Roman Governor of Judea (Acts 24:24).

Roman Emperors in NT times

Ceasar Augustus	31 BC – AD 14
Tiberius	AD 14–37
Gaius Caligula	37–41
Claudius	41–54
Nero	54–68
Galba	68–69
Vespasian	69–79
Titus	79–81
Domitian	81–96

Only three emperors are mentioned by name in the NT: Jesus was born under Augustus (Luke 2:1) and died under Tiberius (Luke 3:1). The third named emperor is Claudius (Acts 11:28 and 18:2): he expelled the Jews from Rome perhaps because of disturbances among the Jews over the Christian faith. The spread of the early church as recorded in the Book of Acts took place during the reigns of Caligula, Claudius and Nero.

Both Nero and later Domitian persecuted the church. Nero's persecution (c. AD 64–68) was largely confined to Rome and was in the latter part of his reign. Tradition has it that Peter and Paul were put to death on his orders, but this is not recorded in the Bible. Many think that the number 666 in Revelation 13:18 is a coded reference to Nero. Some NT letters have Nero's persecution as their backdrop, for example, the First Peter, written from 'Babylon' (1 Pet 5:13), a code-word for Rome.

Domitian's persecution (c. AD 90–96) was more widespread and threatening. He insisted that everyone, even Christians, call him 'lord and god', something believers could not do with a clear conscience. Domitian's persecution is the likely background to the last book of the Bible, Revelation.

Roman procurators
Rome appointed procurators – or governors – to administer the province of Judea. Three are mentioned in the NT:

Pontius Pilate	AD 26–36	He ordered Jesus' crucifixion
Marcus Antonius Felix	c. AD 52–59	Acts 23–24
Porcius Festus	c. AD 59–62	Acts 25–26

The last two kept Paul in prison and put him on trial.

Parables of Jesus

	Matthew	Mark	Luke
Lamp under a bowl	5:14–16	4:21–23	8:16; 11:33
Wise and foolish builders	7:24–27		6:46–49
New patch on an old coat	9:16	2:21	5:36
New wine in old wineskins	9:17	2:22	5:37–39
Sower, seed and different soils	13:3–9,18–23	4:3–8, 13–20	8:4–8,11–15
Weeds among wheat	13:24–30, 36–43		
Mustard seed	13:31–32	4:30–32	13:18–19
Yeast	13:33		13:20–21
Buried treasure	13:44		
Priceless pearl	13:45–46		
Fishing net	13:47–50		
Treasure old and new	13:52		
Lost sheep	18:12–14		15:3–7
Unforgiving servant	18:21–35		
Workers in the vineyard	20:1–16		
Two sons	21:28–32		
Wicked tenants in the vineyard	21:33–41	12:1–9	20:9–16
Wedding invitation	22:1–14		
Fig tree heralding summer	24:32–33	13:28	21:29–30
Good and bad servants	24:45–51		12:42–48
Ten bridesmaids	25:1–13		
Talents (pounds)	25:14–30		19:12–27
Sheep & goats	25:31–46		
Growing seed		4:26–29	
Money–lender			7:41–50
Good Samaritan			10:30–37
Friend at midnight			11:5–8
Rich fool			12:16–21
Watchful servants			12:35–40
Barren fig tree			13:6–9
Humility and honour			14:7–14
Great banquet			14:16–24
Counting the cost			14:28–33

	Matthew	Mark	Luke
Lost coin			15:8–10
Lost (prodigal) son and his brother			15:11–32
Shrewd manager			16:1–8
Rich man and Lazarus			16:19–31
Master and servant			17:7–10
Widow and judge			18:1–8
Pharisee and tax–collector			18:10–14

Miracles of Jesus

	Matthew	Mark	Luke	John
Miracles of healing:				
Demonised man in synagogue		1:23–26	4:33–35	
Royal official's son				4:46–54
Peter's mother-in-law	8:14–15	1:30–31	4:38–39	
Leper	8:2–4	1:40–45	5:12–14	
Paralysed man	9:2–7	2:3–12	5:18–25	
Invalid at Pool of Bethsaida				5:1–9
Man with withered hand	12:10–13	3:1–5	6:6–10	
Demonised man (Legion)	8:28–34	5:1–15	8:27–35	
Woman with haemorrhage	9:20–22	5:25–34	8:43–48	
Two blind men	9:27–31			
Man dumb and demonised	9:32–33			
Gentile woman's daughter	15:21–28	7:24–30		
Deaf and dumb man		7:31–37		
Blind man at Bethsaida		8:22–26		
Epileptic boy with demon	17:14–18	9:17–29	9:38–43	
Man blind from birth				9:1–41
Man dumb, blind and demonised	12:22		11:14	
Crippled woman			13:11–13	
Man with dropsy			14:1–4	
Ten lepers			17:11–19	
Blind Bartimaeus (and another)	20:29–34	10:46–52	18:35–43	
High priest servant's ear			22:50–51	

	Matthew	Mark	Luke	John
Power over death:				
Centurion's dying servant	8:5–13		7:1–10	
Widow's son (at Nain)			7:11–15	
Jairus' daughter	9:18–19, 23–25	5:22–24, 35–43	8:41–42, 49–56	
Lazarus				11:1–44
Power over nature:				
Water into wine				2:1–11
Calming of the storm	8:23–27	4:37–41	8:22–25	
Walking on water	14:22–33	6:48–51		6:19–21
Feeding of the 5,000	14:15–21	6:35–44	9:12–17	6:5–13
Feeding of the 4,000	15:32–38	8:1–9		
Coin found in fish	17:24–27			
Fig-tree withered	21:18–22	11:12–14, 20–24		
Catch of fish			5:1–11	
Another catch of fish				21:1–11

Old Testament prophecy fulfilled in Christ

Here are a few examples of Old Testament prophecies in which New Testament writers find an anticipation of Jesus Christ whom they regard as the Messiah:

His birth in Bethlehem:	Mic 5:2	Matt 2:1–6; Luke 2:4–6
His birth to a virgin	Isa 7:14	Matt 1:18–25; Luke 1:26–38
His birth more generally	Isa 9:6–7; 11:1	
His flight to Egypt	Hos 11:1	Matt 2:13–15
His ministry of compassion	Isa 61:1,2	Luke 4:16–21
His entry into Jerusalem	Zech 9:9	Matt 21:1–9; John 12:12–15
His rejection by his own people	Isa 53:1–3	Matt 26:3,4; John 12:37–43
	see Ps 118:22,23	Acts 4:11, 1 Pet 2:7
His betrayal by Judas	Ps 41:9	Matt 26:14–16, 47–50; John 13:18

His value set at 30 silver pieces	Zech 11:12,13	Matt 27:9,10
His abandonment by the disciples	Zech 13:7	Matt 26:31; Mark 14:27
His trial and conviction	Isa 53:8	Matt 27:1,2; Luke 23:1–25
His silence on trial	Isa 53:7	Matt 27:12–14; Mark 15:3–5; Luke 23:8–10
He was struck and spat upon	Isa 50:6	Matt 26:67; 27:30; Mark 14:65
He was mocked and insulted	Ps 22:7,8	Matt 27:39–44; Luke 23:11,35
He was crucified	Ps 22:14,16,17	Matt 27:31; Mark 15:20,25
He died with criminals	Isa 53:12	Matt 27:38; Mark 15:27,28; Luke 23:32–34
He was offered vinegar	Ps 69:21	Matt 27:34; John 19:28–30
His cloak was gambled for	Ps 22:18	Matt 27:35; John 19:23,24
His bones were unbroken	Exod 12:46	John 19:31–36
He died for sin	Isa 53	John 1:29; 2 Cor 5:21
He felt forsaken by God	Ps 22:1	Matt 27:46; Mk 15:34
He was raised to life	Ps 16:10	Matt 28:1–10; Acts 2:24–28; 13:35
He is now at God's right hand	Ps 110:1	Mark 16:19; Luke 24:50,51; Heb 1:13

Old Testament quotes in the New

Altogether there are around 260 Old Testament quotations in the New. Nearly all Bibles use footnotes to indicate where they come from. Ninety come from the Pentateuch (Genesis to

Deuteronomy); fifty from Isaiah, thirty from the minor prophets and over seventy from the Psalms.

Most Old Testament quotations that appear in the New are taken from the Greek translation of the Old Testament known as the Septuagint (LXX). This explains why the wording may not be exactly the same.

Jesus quoted nineteen Old Testament books and referred by name to twenty Old Testament characters. The Gospel of Mark has thirty-three OT quotations; Luke and John around forty each; while Matthew has no fewer than seventy.

Bible facts & figures (Authorized Version)

	Old Testament	New Testament
Books	39	27
Chapters	929	289
Verses	23,214	7,959
Words	593,493	181,253
Shortest book	Obadiah	Second John
Longest book (in words)	Jeremiah	Acts
Shortest verse	1 Chron 1:25	John 11:35

Glossary of Bible words & phrases
* refers to a cross-reference

Abba
An Aramaic word meaning 'father' or 'daddy'. Both intimate and respectful. Used of God the Father in three places: Mark 14:36; Rom 8:15; Gal 4:6.

Apostle
Someone sent on a mission. Jesus designated his disciples 'apostles' (Mark 3:14). Paul was the Apostle to the Gentiles (Acts 9:15; 22:21; 26:23; Rom 11:13; Gal 2:7,8).

Angel
A supernatural being. They surround God's throne and can also be sent by God to do his bidding. The word 'angel' means 'messenger'. In the Bible they appear in various guises and for various purposes (see Acts 7:53; 2 Cor 11:14; Gal 3:19; Heb 1:14; 13:2). The expression 'the angel of the Lord' refers to the appearance of God in visible form. Cherubs* and seraphs* were special types of angel.

Ark of the covenant, ark of the testimony
A chest made of acacia wood measuring 112 cm long, 67 cm high and 67 cm wide, kept in the innermost part of the Tent of Meeting* and later the temple*. It contained various holy items and symbolised the presence of God. When outside, it was carried on poles. Not to be confused with Noah's ark.

Asherah and Ashteroth
See Baal*

Baal (or Ba'al)
A general name (meaning 'master') for several of the pagan deities worshipped by Canaanites and others. Baal worship often included fertility rites. Baal, being male, was linked in worship to the female goddesses Asherah and Ashteroth. Worship of these so-called gods was often associated with special 'high places' ie hill-top shrines. The prophet Elijah won a contest on Mount Carmel against the prophets of Baal and Asherah (1 Kings 18).

Baptism
The immersion into water as a sign of God's cleansing from sin. It became for Christians a means of declaring their faith in Christ. Today, some churches practise infant baptism, others only the baptism of believing adults.

Beelzebub, or Beelzebul
A name given to Satan* as leader of the evil spirits (Matt 9:34; 10:25; Luke 11:15). Perhaps linked to the name of an earlier Philistine god (2 Kings 1:2,3).

Behemoth
See Leviathan*.

Bless
People can bless God, ie bestow thanks upon him. Or God can bless people, ie bestow his favour upon them. In the Beatitudes (Matt 5:3–10), the 'blessed' have reason to be happy in the Lord.

Cherub (plural: cherubs or cherubim)
A winged angel. Cherubs guarded Eden (Gen 3:24). Later, representations of cherubs stood over the Ark of the Covenant* (Exod 25–27, 1 Kings 6). Ezekiel had several visions containing cherubs. See also seraph*.

Christ
The Greek form of 'Messiah'.*

Church
The Greek word is *ekklesia*. It means an assembly or gathering. William Tyndale, an early Bible translator, preferred the rendering 'congregation'.

Circumcise, circumcision
The removal of the foreskin from the penis of a male Jew. Usually carried out when one week old. A sign of God's covenant with Abraham and the Israelites (see Gen 17:9–14).

Concubine
An extra 'wife' which a man took either as a means of having children or, in the case of royalty, for sexual gratification and/or as a way of making an alliance with another nation.

Covenant

An agreement between two people, two nations or, most often in the Bible, between God and his people. A covenant sets out the terms and conditions of the agreement, together with the penalties for breaking it and the blessings for keeping it.

Covet, coveting

To crave what belongs to someone else. Forbidden in the last of the Ten Commandments.

Crucify, crucifixion

To put to death by means of nailing or tying a person to a cross of wood. One of the cruellest and most degrading forms of execution ever invented. Used by the Romans.

'Day of the Lord'

The time of God's judgement on the wicked and his salvation for the faithful. Many Old Testament prophets give warnings about the 'Day of the Lord'.

Deacon

A church officer, junior to an elder*. Described in 1 Tim 3. The word means 'one who serves'.

Demon, demoniac

See evil spirit*.

Divination

The practice of seeking guidance by means forbidden by God (Lev 19:26; Deut 18:10, 11, 14). Another name for fortune-telling.

Elder

A church officer. Generally a person of mature spiritual quality. Described in 1 Tim 3, Titus 1 and 1 Pet 5. Interchangeable with 'overseer'.

Elect, election

To choose. God is said to have chosen the nation Israel. A believer is said to be chosen in Christ (see John 15:16). The word speaks of God's initiative in his saving work. (See Deut 7:7,8; 9:4–5; John 15:16; Rom 9:18–29; Eph 1:4; 1 Pet 2:9.)

Ephod
A word with various meanings. However, it most commonly refers to a breastpiece worn by the High Priest and containing the Urim and Thummin* (Exodus 28)

Eunuch
A castrated man. Often employed to guard a monarch's harem. The Law forbade a eunuch from becoming a full convert to Judaism (Deut 23:1). However, Philip led an Ethiopian eunuch to full faith in Christ (Acts 8:26–39).

Evil spirits
Otherwise known as unclean* spirits or demons. Supernatural powers, agents of Satan, partially or wholly controlling a person and causing defilement, sometimes illness. Someone under the influence of a demon is known as a demoniac. The most serious case Jesus dealt with was that of Legion (Matt 8:28–34; Mark 5:1–15; Luke 8:27–35).

Faith
In its weaker sense, faith can mean simply to believe that something is true; in its stronger sense it means to put one's complete trust and undivided loyalty in someone. In the NT, Christian teaching is sometimes called 'the faith' (Gal 1:23; Eph 4:5; Jude 3).

Fast, fasting
The practice of going without food as a spiritual discipline. Jesus fasted for forty days before commencing his public ministry (Matthew 4:1,2; Luke 4:1,2).

Gehenna
A word sometimes translated 'hell'.*

Gentile
Anyone who is not Jewish, meaning 'belonging to the nations'. The Jews called Gentiles 'dogs'. Paul was a missionary to the Gentiles.

Grace
God's undeserved love and kindness.

Hades
Greek equivalent to the Hebrew 'sheol'*.

Hell
It can translate one of several Greek words. The most significant is Gehenna*. Geographically, this refers to the Valley of Hinnom outside Jerusalem in which child-sacrifice once took place. Spiritually, it refers to eternal destruction and punishment. Jesus said more about hell than anyone else in the Bible.

Holy, holiness
If something is 'holy', it is set apart for God, consecrated for his use. God's holiness is what distinguishes him from sinful human beings. God is called the Holy One.

Holy of holies
The inner sanctum of the Tabernacle*, later the temple*. The area was curtained off and only the High Priest was allowed to enter on very special occasions. Also known as the Most Holy Place.

Horn of salvation
'Horn' found in more traditional translations, means strength. Hence, 'horn of salvation' means God's saving strength or his saving power.

Idol, idolatry
An idol is a man-made construction of a false god. Idolatry, forbidden in the Ten Commandments, is the worship of such gods. Paul says that to covet anything is to turn it into an idol (Col 3:5).

Iniquity
Wrongdoing, wickedness. The word means to depart from God's standards in the way that a wall might depart from the true vertical. Used mostly in more formal translations.

Jehovah
An old spelling for Yahweh (YHWH).*

Justify, justification
To be put right with God. A good way to think of the meaning of justification is to remember that when God forgives us it is *just-as-if* we never sinned.

Kingdom of God, kingdom of heaven
Not a physical place, but wherever God's authority is accepted. Jesus

spoke of people entering the kingdom. Sometimes, he described the kingdom as being present, at other times as still being future.

Law
God's requirements of human beings. Other Bible words, each with a subtle difference in meaning, include commandment, statute, ordinance and precept.

Laying on of hands
In the OT the act symbolises: (1) the parental bestowal of inheritance rights; (2) appointment to an office; and (3) the placing of one's sin and guilt on an animal. In the NT it symbolises: (1) the bestowal of blessing (Matt 19:13,15; see Luke 24:50); (2) the means of miraculous healing (Matt 9:18; Mark 16:18; Acts 9:12,17; James 5:14,15); (3) the outpouring of the Holy Spirit (Acts 8:17,19; 19:6); and (4) recognition of a call to serve God in some way (Acts 6:6; 13:3; 1 Tim 4:14; 2 Tim 1:6).

Leprosy, leper
Both the disease of that name, but also other skin diseases. Leprosy made a person unclean and lepers were treated as outcasts. In the OT, Naaman of Syria was cured of leprosy (2 Kings 5). Jesus healed lepers more than once.

Leviathan
A (legendary?) water animal. Job 41 and elsewhere. Also called Rahab or Behemoth.

Lord
Spelt with capital letters, this is how most English Bible translations render the Hebrew word 'Yahweh'*.

Lord of Hosts
A title for God frequently found in the OT and stressing his power. Hosts means armies. All powers, both natural and supernatural are at God's disposal.

Manna
Heavenly food that God gave the Israelites as they wandered in the desert (Exodus 16:14–32).

Messiah
God's appointed. The one on whom God's power and blessing rests, the one chosen to carry out God's work of salvation. Hebrew equivalent of the Greek Christ.

Parable
A story with a purpose. Parables usually have one main point. See the list of Jesus' parables earlier in this chapter.

Pharisee
See 'Jewish religious and political parties' earlier in this chapter.

Predestine, predestination
To decide in advance. Christians are said to be predestined by God for salvation (Rom 8:29,30; Eph 1:5,11).

Publican
An old word for tax collector. See 'Jewish religious and political parties' earlier in this chapter.

Ransom
The price paid to redeem*.

Reconcile, reconciliation
To bring two enemies together. However, it is we who need to be reconciled to God, not God who needs to be reconciled to us. Jesus is our means of reconciliation. (Rom 5:11; 2 Cor 5:18,19).

Redeem, redeemer, redemption
To buy back. The word is most often used of someone sold into slavery. God redeemed his people from their slavery in Egypt. The Christian is redeemed because Christ has paid the price – his death – for us to be redeemed out of slavery to sin.

Remnant
The faithful few of God's people who were left after the rest had been killed or taken into captivity.

Repent, repentance
To turn back to God and away from wrongdoing. Literally, to change one's mind.

Righteous, righteousness
Good, meeting with God's approval. Obeying God's laws. Upright.

Sabbath
A weekly day of rest. God rested on the seventh day after making the world (Gen 2:2,3) and commanded his people to rest on one day each week (Exod 20:8–11).

Sadducee
See 'Jewish religious and political parties' earlier in this chapter.

Saints
Not special Christians, as in the modern sense, but any believer (eg Phil 1:1). People who are 'set apart' for God's service. It means 'holy ones'.

Samaritan
In NT times, the Samaritans occupied a region between the two Jewish provinces of Judea and Galilee. They probably descended from the few Israelites left behind when Assyria destroyed northern Israel in 722 BC. These intermarried with newcomers of other nationalities moved into the region by the Assyrians. The Samaritans adopted an impure form of the Jewish faith: they did not worship in Jerusalem, but had their own temple on Mount Gerizim.

The Samaritans were hated by the Jews who went out of their way to avoid them. Jesus spoke to an unnamed Samaritan woman at Sychar (John 4). He also told the Parable of the Good Samaritan (Luke 10:30–37).

After Pentecost, Philip preached the Gospel in Samaria (Acts 8).

Sanctify, sanctification
To make holy*.

Sanhedrin
The Jewish High Council. See 'Jewish religious and political parties' earlier in this chapter.

Satan
One name for the devil, meaning 'accuser' or 'opponent'. Mentioned rarely in the OT (Job 1,2; Zech 3:1,2), but more often in the NT. His destruction is assured because of Christ's victory on the Cross.

Saviour, salvation
Salvation is the process of being saved or rescued from some disaster. Jesus Christ is our Saviour.

Scribe
See 'Jewish religious and political parties' earlier in this chapter.

Selah
A technical word that appears in some psalms, perhaps meaning 'pause' or 'repeat'.

Seraph (plural: seraphs or seraphim)
A six-winged angel.* They appear only in Isaiah 6. See cherub*.

Sheol
A Hebrew word describing the grave or the place of the dead. In the OT there was only a poorly developed understanding of the afterlife. For the most part, only a shadowy existence after death was imagined. The Greek equivalent is Hades*.

Sin
Wrongdoing. To fall short, rather like an arrow falling short of its target (see Rom 3:23). Compare with 'iniquity'* and 'transgression'.*

Son of Man
Jesus' favourite title for himself. It can mean simply 'mortal man', as in Ezekiel. But Jesus had in mind Daniel 7:13,14, which describes a messianic figure given God's power and authority. Jesus claimed the Son of Man could forgive sin (Mark 2:10) and would stand in judgement (John 5:27).

Tabernacle or Tent of meeting
The Tent that was used as a portable place of worship while the Israelites wandered in the desert (Exod 25–31; 35–40)

Temple
See under 'Places of Worship' towards the beginning of this chapter.

Testament
Another word for covenant*. The Bible is divided into the Old and New Testaments.

Tithe
A tenth part of one's income or possessions, made as a gift to God.

Tetrarch
See Herod's family tree earlier in this chapter.

Transgress, transgression
To break the law. The word means to cross the line. Compare with 'sin'.*

Unclean
Ceremonially impure, defiled. Certain foods were unclean and people were unclean under certain conditions. Evil spirits are called 'unclean' spirits.

Unleavened bread
Bread made without yeast to act as a raising agent; therefore flat. Eaten at Passover.

Urim and Thummin
Two small objects used by the priest in consulting God and determining his will. Kept in the priest's ephod*.

Watchman
A person standing on a tower or city wall to keep a look out for the arrival of messengers or advancing enemy troops.

Yahweh (YHWH)
The Hebrew name for God. It means 'I am' (Exod 3:14)

Zealot
See 'Jewish religious and political parties' earlier in this chapter.

Zion, daughter of Zion
Zion was the hill on which Jerusalem and its Temple stood. Sometimes used interchangeably with Jerusalem or metaphorically for the worshipping community.